THE IMAGE OF LEADERSHIP IN SALES

Special Edition, 10th Anniversary

THE IMAGE OF LEADERSHIP IN SALES

How Leaders in Sales Package Themselves
to Stand Out for All the Right Reasons

by
Sylvie di Giusto

Copyright © 2024 Sylvie di Giusto LLC
All rights reserved

No part of this book may be reproduced in any form or by any electronic or mechanical means, including information storage and retrieval systems, without permission in writing from the author. The only exception is by a reviewer, who may quote short excerpts in a published review.

The information presented herein represents the views of the author as of the date of publication. This book is presented for informational purposes only. Because of the rate at which conditions change, the author reserves the right to alter and update her opinions at any time. Although every attempt has been made to verify the information in this book, the author does not assume any responsibility for errors, inaccuracies, or omissions.

ISBN: 979-8-9901927-3-7

To the deal-makers and masters of negotiations
whose courage to drive sales and reshape markets
is fueled by their commitment to understanding
and valuing every client interaction.

Contents

About This Special Edition 9
Foreword by Mark Hunter 12
Introduction 18
Chapter 1: Seven Seconds 24
    The Cost of a Poor Professional Imprint 36
Chapter 2: Your Professional Imprint 46
    The Science of First Impressions 52
    The Sustained Imprint 57
    The Invisible Filters of Perception 63
    Stand Out for the Right Reasons 74
    When Details Speak Loudest 78
    The ABCDEs of Your Professional Identity 85
    Internal and External Consistency 90
Chapter 3: Leaders Look Confident 96
    Leaders Are Confident about Their Body 103
    Leaders Are Confident about Their Age 108
    Leaders Are Confident about Their Gender Identity 111
    Leaders Are Confident about Their Style 115
Chapter 4: Leaders Look Authentic 120
    Keywords Are the Keys to Authenticity 124
    The Explorer: Approachable and Relaxed 129
    The Traditionalist: Trustworthy and Reliable 131
    The Cosmopolitan: Sophisticated and Eloquent 133
    The Caregiver: Supportive and Nurturing 137
    The Avant-Garde: Individualistic and Creative 139
    The Glamorous: Magnetic and Extravagant 141
    The Dramatic: Strong and Fearless 143

Chapter 5: Leaders Look Professional 150
Prescribed Uniformity in Action 157
Silent Standards and Unwritten Uniforms 160
Internal Mandates We Self-Enforce 164
Dressing Beyond the Code: Situational Awareness 172

Chapter 6: Leaders Look Respectful 178
It's a Sign of Self-Respect 181
It Shows You Respect Others 186
It's Not Always Reciprocated 191

Chapter 7: Leaders Look Controlled 196
Self-Awareness and Self-Reflection 198
Self-Care and Self-Discipline 199
Self-Improvement and Self-Promotion 200
Be Prepared for the Predictable and the Unpredictable 203
It's Not Only about Clothes 205

Chapter 8: Leadership in a Digital Landscape 216
KNOW: Assessing the Scope of Your e-Shadow 220
REPAIR: Correcting Your Cyber Image 222
OWN: Claiming Your Virtual Real Estate 224
CONTROL: Commanding Your Digital Boundaries 225
MONITOR: Persistent Surveillance of Your Online Self 226

Chapter 9: Leaders Lead by Example 230
The Leader's Challenge: It's Not You, It's Someone Else 232

Chapter 10: Moving Forward 242

Acknowledgments 247

About the Author 249

Perception Audit 250

Your Voice and Our Collective Reach 251

About This Special Edition

Ten years ago I released *The Image of Leadership*, not fully grasping the impact it would have on my own career trajectory. At that time I remember feeling a mix of excitement and nervousness. After all, releasing a book into the world is no small feat. Just a few weeks before I hit that "Publish" button and while I was still overthinking every single word, Mark Sanborn, a titan of leadership thought and Hall of Fame speaker himself, gave me a piece of advice that has stayed with me: "Nobody cares about your first book, but everybody cares that you have a first book." In the speaking world, a book is an entry point, a business card, a conversation starter, a testament to your thoughts and expertise. So I published mine.

That book did, indeed, open doors and spark conversations, fulfilling its role perfectly—and much more. But Mark wasn't finished after his original words. He turned and, while walking off, threw a greater challenge my way: "But you really must write a good second book, Sylvie." So consider this special edition of *The Image of Leadership for Sales* my "second good book," the refined version of my initial offering.

You see, a lot has changed in ten years. The digital landscape has evolved rapidly with the rise of mobile technology, cloud computing, and artificial intelligence transforming the way we work and connect. Social media not only has reshaped our personal connections, it has revolutionized marketing and customer engagement strategies. Casual work attire has become more accepted, reflecting a shift toward prioritizing comfort and individuality in the workplace. Diversity and inclusion have taken center stage with a growing recognition of the importance of creating equitable work environments. The global marketplace has become increasingly interconnected, requiring leaders to navigate cultural differences and build international relationships. And we can't forget the profound impact of the pandemic that accelerated the adoption of remote work, virtual collaboration, and digital transformation. It was clear that *The Image of Leadership* needed more than just a touch-up—it needed a full makeover to reflect these seismic shifts and provide guidance for leaders navigating this new landscape.

The book needed a comprehensive renewal to stay relevant in a world that has fundamentally shifted. And so I embarked on a journey of complete revision rather than superficial changes. This wasn't just about updating; it was about reimagining and realigning the book with the times we live in.

In that revision process I made a conscious decision to dedicate several special editions to the incredible individuals I've met and spoken to over the years. As a keynote speaker, the exchange is a two-way street. For every insight I've offered from the stage, I've received an equal measure of wisdom from my prospects or clients and my audiences. The specific challenges they've shared, the questions they've asked, and the stories they've told have enriched my understanding of and approach to leadership.

I'm immensely thankful for this reciprocal learning. It's this exchange that has breathed new life into *The Image of Leadership*, transforming it into a special edition that reflects not just my voice but the collective voice of the many dedicated professionals I've had the honor to engage with.

This special edition is dedicated to you, the sales leaders who serve a wide variety of industries. It addresses the unique challenges and triumphs you face daily in your professional sales arenas. But it's more than just an update; it's a recommitment to the principles of leadership tailored to the nuances of your experiences where the stakes are high, and the demands are varied across industries.

Here's to you, the sales leaders who embody resilience and dedication every day. This book is for you—the ethical, the passionate, the determined. Whether you're navigating the complex world of B2B enterprise sales, crafting personalized experiences in B2C retail, pioneering new frontiers in e-commerce and D2C, or building lasting relationships through consultative selling, this book is a testament to your unwavering commitment.

And this book is a resource for sales professionals at every level, from the tenacious Sales Development Representatives making their first calls to the visionary Chief Revenue Officers steering their organizations to new heights. It's a guide for those in the trenches of technology, financial services, healthcare, manufacturing, media sales—any industry where the stakes are high and the challenges are unique.

In addition, this book is a celebration of the diverse methodologies and approaches you employ, from the art of solution selling to the science of data-driven decision-making, from the nuance of social selling to the empathy of customer-centric strategies.

It's also a thank-you for your service across industries and a tool to aid your journey forward, whether you're engaging with prospects or clients face-to-face, over the phone, online, or in the boardroom. It's a recognition of the sales leaders who are shaping the future, one relationship at a time.

Consider this book the "second" that Mark Sanborn urged me to perfect, a version refined by experience and honed by the passage of time. It's a handbook for the present, a road map for the future, and a testament to the enduring power of a leader's image that transcends the diverse landscapes of sales.

May this special edition serve as a beacon through the ever-changing landscape of leadership in sales, inspiring you to continue making impactful decisions with confidence, purpose, and authority as you navigate the unique challenges of interacting with prospects or clients and drive success in your role as the leader of a sales team.

Foreword
by Mark Hunter

Sales is leadership and leadership is sales. I've used this phrase for years because of a simple truth, there's no difference between the two. Show me a great leader who does not "sell" their vision to the people they're leading. They simply can't exist. Show me a great salesperson, and you'll see a person who is leading their customer. The two are truly interchangeable.

The challenge is understanding what it means to lead. Anyone can say they're leading, but that doesn't mean anything. Leadership today is far more complex than ever before. We live in a highly visible world and this alone is one reason why being a leader is more difficult than ever.

When Sylvie provided me the manuscript for this book and asked me to write the foreword, I felt honored, as her book is truly a marriage of two key activities, sales and leadership. There are numerous books that have been written about leadership and I suppose an equal number on sales. Why more have not been written about the two together is something I'll never understand. We can be thankful Sylvie took on the challenge and did it in a masterful way.

The mastery in the book is knowing the author. I can't remember when or where I first met Sylvie, but it was years ago. In every interaction I've had with her, I see this book being lived out. This is the brilliance of the book; it's not a book of facts, but one that is a self-portrait of Sylvie and who she is.

The content is 100% congruent with her as a person, and this is why chapter 4 is titled, "Leaders Look Authentic." Few people could write this book, and Sylvie is one of those few. I'm glad she chose to write this, and so will you after you've finished.

As you read this book, do so with a notebook in hand or your phone ready to take notes. As you read, allow your mind to create visual images of your customers, yourself, and whether they align.

Time is not on the side of the sales leader, in fact time works against the sales leader. Sylvie does a great job in the book explaining the 7-second rule and how it will make or destroy a salesperson, or anyone else. I'm sure your mother shared with you as a child the importance of making a first impression, I know mine did many, many times. Growing up, my mother would emphasize how the first impression could be the lasting impression. The challenge is, this first impression goes far beyond how we might introduce ourselves and the first words out of our mouth. Sylvie details in this book the damage a bad first impression can have.

What this book does so well is help us see how our success in sales begins with us. We send off so many signals—many unbeknownst to us—but very visible to the customer. There's a reason why sometimes we can walk into a sales meeting and the customer is eager to do business with us. Our reputation arrives before we do, and it's much more than what we sell. Customers have choices; they don't have to do business with us, but they choose to for many reasons, and the first is us. Are we a person they want to work with?

A few years ago I was working with a company that was struggling, their sales weren't growing. The CEO shared how they struggled with customers walking away, a sales cycle that was lengthening, and worst of all, declining profit margins. He was adamant they had to find better customers. He was right, they did have to find better customers, but the solution would only occur when they hired different salespeople.

There's a simple premise we have to realize about human nature. We do business with people who are either like us or people who we aspire to be. What this company had was salespeople who failed to understand the power they had in shaping the business. The salesforce, and in particular their leadership, lacked professionalism in how they handled themselves. They didn't hold themselves accountable, but rather would blame everything else.

During multiple conversations with the CEO and senior sales leaders, I saw each person putting on a mask, not willing to own up to the challenge and accept the role they had in fixing it. The result was zero openness to work together as a team. The communication that did take place was hostile and blame-filled.

Was I successful in turning them around? No, but I was successful in finding another company to buy them out. Immediately upon closing the sale, the entire sales leadership team and salesforce was terminated. The new company's salesforce took over and sales began growing. Even with no change in the product or pricing, sales began to grow rapidly. Why? It's simple, the new salesforce understood the importance of creating the right impression and creating a professional environment where customers wanted to do business with the new salespeople.

Sales can be tough, or at least that's what a lot of people say, especially when it comes to finding new customers. Ask any salesperson what part of sales they like the least and they will most likely say prospecting.

To help put this into perspective, my daughter is a nurse. On a flight, another passenger began having seizures and my daughter, being trained as a nurse, immediately stepped in to help. She didn't hesitate, she saw a passenger in need and immediately began assisting. This is exactly what prospecting is all about. If you have the ability to help someone you owe it to them to reach out.

Look around at who you could serve, do you believe you could help them? If the answer is "yes" then you owe it to them. In fact if you don't reach out, you're doing them a disservice. Was the passenger on the plane thankful for my daughter's assistance? Of course they were. The same with the customers we get to serve. I'm not saying what we do is anything close to a life or death situation like my daughter faced, but the parallel is the same. We owe it to others to reach out and help.

Salespeople who are successful at prospecting are the ones who believe in themselves. They understand the importance of not just the first impression, but every aspect of the sales process. Sales is much more than exchanging money for goods or services. Sales is about helping others see and achieve what they didn't think was possible.

Read that last sentence again, very slowly. You're now in a position to help others. Your success in sales is never going to occur until you first believe in yourself and understand your impact. You could have the best solution in the marketplace, it could be something the customer desperately needs but you'll never get the chance if the customer fails to believe in you.

A few years ago I was working with a high-end automotive company. I was charged with increasing the number of automobiles moved per month in each of their locations across the country. The challenge was the automobiles sold for well in excess of $100,000, yet their salespeople could barely afford a $40,000 car. You can see the disconnect—the salespeople could not see the value in the 100K+ plus vehicle. The automotive company had provided countless hours of technical training on each model. Every salesperson could recite hundreds of facts regarding how the automobile operated, drove, etc. Despite a huge investment in product training, the sales results didn't budge.

I came in and shifted the focus to understanding the customer, learning how to communicate with them, how to see things through their eyes. The focus was on the customer, not the vehicle. An interesting thing began to happen; turnover of salespeople decreased, sales increased, and what I took real pleasure in is how both the customer and the salesperson began to enjoy the new car buying experience.

Why did this occur? Yes, the sales team was now focused on the customer, but it was also because the salesperson was finally engaging with the customer and doing it on their terms. I only wish I had Sylvie's book at that time and could have provided each salesperson with a copy. I'm sure the results they would have achieved would have been even higher.

There's something magical when we connect with the customer. Not only do we wind up closing more sales, but also we open up additional doors. In fact, I wish we would never use the phrase "closing more sales" again. Rather than closing more sales, I'd prefer to "open more relationships" and allow those relationships to create more opportunities to serve people. When we believe in ourselves and follow each principle laid out in this book to create meaningful relationships, we will do just that—open more opportunities.

Sales is not a dirty word, it's a beautiful word. We as the sales community have allowed a few bad apples to create the notion that sales is a dirty word. If sales is a dirty word, then we have to wonder where the economy would be without salespeople? Nothing happens until somebody sells something. The global economy would grind to a halt if business had nobody to sell to. We as salespeople serve a key role in the marketplace. We can't look at it as a something we have to do, rather something we get to do.

Our potential as a sales leader knows no limits, and this is a key reason why I love sales. Your success, and my success are only constrained by the parameters we put on it.

Early on in my sales career I didn't feel this way. To me sales was merely a job. I had specific tasks to do and I did them, albeit never to the potential I should have. The reason was simple, I viewed sales as merely the thing I had to do to earn the money I needed to live.

Several years into my sales career I had a boss who was patient enough to show me what sales was. It was not the transactional activity I thought, but rather it was about relationships and helping people. My boss stressed how sales begins with me.

He shared countless stories of other salespeople he trained over the years, some who became incredibly successful and others who flamed out and moved on. With each story of a successful salesperson came the full breakdown of what he or she did to ensure they connected with each customer. My boss was detailed in explaining the results these people achieved.

It didn't take me long to connect the dots. If I wanted to be successful in sales I first had to invest in myself and ensure everything about me measured up. In time, I saw the more I invested in growing myself personally and professionally, the greater the results I was achieving. Over time I no longer saw sales as a job full of tasks to do, but rather connections I was honored to make. Sales was no longer a job, nor a profession, sales had become a lifestyle.

You may read this and say you're not buying into that belief. Go ahead and be a skeptic—I was—but over the course of several years I began to buy in. Decades later, I'm still buying in, in fact I'm buying in more each year. How could I not? When I see sales as helping others, how can I not get excited!? Go ahead, try it, throw yourself into the deep end of the sales pool and call me in a couple of years. I'll expect to hear how you've come to see sales not as a job, not as a profession, but as a lifestyle just as I do.

The next step is now yours to take. Read the book, apply the book. The world needs sales leaders, not merely those who have it in their title, but those who live it. Regardless of your position in the sale food chain, from entry-level salesperson to Chief Revenue Officer, we are all sales leaders.

Mark Hunter
The Sales Hunter

Introduction

Welcome to *The Image of Leadership in Sales*. The title reflects the reality that every sales leader should acknowledge—that true leadership manifests itself in two equally vital ways— the seen and the unseen. Even though all leaders have their own individual styles and personalities, it cannot be doubted that the leaders who succeed over a long period are seen and accepted because their interior skills and exterior images are effectively aligned. In other words, what you see is what you get. As leaders, they're consistent and dependable, and their professional imprint—which I'll introduce to you later in the book—is strong and durable.

Whether you are masterfully navigating the intricate corridors of B2B sales, advocating for client needs within the structured area of account management, enriching customer experiences in the retail industry, driving transformative initiatives in the world of e-commerce, or boldly pioneering innovative ventures as a sales entrepreneur, you may wonder if this book is for you.

It is. It's definitely for you. It's crafted not only for the seasoned sales executive and the aspiring leader but for those who find themselves in competitive industries where the dynamics present a unique set of challenges and opportunities. Regardless of the landscape, whether you stand as a solitary figure in a boardroom or as part of a growing legion of sales leaders, this book is a beacon for your journey that illuminates the ways you can solidify your professional identity and shape your leadership narrative. It's designed to instill a culture of excellence and leadership at every level.

The principles laid out here hold true across all levels of leadership because advancement is a constant pursuit, whether you're a seasoned leader aiming for a top sales executive position, a mid-level professional eyeing a strategic leap into senior management, or starting your leadership journey with aspirations for a pivotal role. As a sales professional in the workplace, you must proactively cultivate and embody the qualities of these roles well in advance, often navigating unique challenges and carving out your path.

Being recognized as having "leadership potential," being someone equipped to manage the upcoming tier of responsibilities and challenges, is essential. The dynamics might differ—navigating the complexities of corporate ladders, mastering the unspoken codes of office politics, or pioneering your own start-up—yet the core principle remains the same: no matter if you're at the threshold of your career or if you're a seasoned professional making pivotal decisions, the way you present yourself should consistently reflect the leader you aspire to be.

The high-stakes negotiations with prospects or clients, the pivotal discussions within team meetings, the charged atmosphere of major deal closings, or the strategic choices made in the executive suite—all these scenarios demand leaders who possess not only the expertise but the professional identity and gravitas to instill confidence and instigate change.

This book will take you step by step through the development of your professional identity. The focus will be on all those things people perceive about you, especially your appearance, your look of leadership. By that I mean your image as you lead a client meeting, speak at a professional sales conference, or articulate your vision in an interview. The book's focus is based on the proven concept that you cannot simply tell others that you're a leader and expect them to treat you as one. You have to show others your leadership, every day, consistently, and in a way that encourages them to quickly accept you as someone they can trust.

One the one hand, this book focuses on how you represent yourself internally to your team or to your own leadership.

On the other hand, remember that all those principles also apply when interacting with a client and extend to all stakeholders. As a leader you are always "on stage," not just in team meetings or when facing your own management. Every interaction matters, whether it's with a colleague in the hallway, a client on a video call, a potential partner at an industry event, or even when you are "off" work, interacting with your community. Your professional identity is constantly being shaped and reinforced by how you present yourself in each of those moments. Remember: everyone is watching you all the time, and your interactions in every situation contribute to the overall perception of your leadership. Only by being mindful of this reality can you ensure that your professional identity is cohesive and impactful, no matter the context.

We'll begin with the seven-second rule, that critical period when others first encounter you. They may have some prior knowledge of you, but this is the first time they actually lay eyes on you. I'll show you how others quickly make up their minds about your leadership potential and either open the door for you or slam it shut. The good thing is that this process is entirely under your control. Already within these first micro moments, you can choose to present yourself as a leader or not.

Hence, I'll reveal the components of your professional imprint and how, after it's been established in those first few seconds, you need to sustain it over time. We'll explore the ABCDEs of your professional imprint—appearance, behavior, communication, digital footprint, and environment.

Although how you dress is vital, this is not a how-to book or fashion guide. I'm not going to detail specific items of clothing or accessories you need to buy and wear. Instead, I want to provide you with a deep understanding of the concepts you need to put into practice in your own way. I want to give you the power to create your own professional identity that is true to your personality, that works for you for the duration of your career, and that stands as a testament to your organization and industry.

We'll also delve into the area of digital leadership. In an age when your digital presence is as crucial as your in-person interactions, we'll explore how to cultivate a compelling digital footprint that reinforces your leadership brand. From leveraging social media platforms to crafting a powerful online narrative, you'll learn strategies to extend your influence and establish yourself as a thought leader in the digital sphere.

Throughout your leadership journey you'll inevitably encounter challenging conversations and situations that test your mettle as a leader. For addressing sensitive issues with team members, I'll equip you with the tools and techniques to approach those difficult conversations with confidence and grace. You'll learn how to communicate with empathy, assert your authority when necessary, and foster a culture of open and constructive dialogue within your team because, as a sales leader, your success is intrinsically tied to your ability to inspire and guide others. Hence, we'll explore the art of leading by example, showcasing how your decisions set the tone for your team and your organization. By embodying the qualities you seek to instill in others, you'll create a ripple effect of positive change.

In crafting this book, it was important to me to recognize that sales professionals' experiences and identities are vast and diverse. That's why this book is committed to embracing all sales leaders, regardless of background or the unique challenges they face in their specific industry or role.

In these pages, every sales leader is welcome and valued.

Leaders come in all genders, shapes, sizes, ages, styles, and levels—including yours. I hope this book will help you develop your professional identity on your journey of becoming the leader you deserve to be. It's all a matter of letting others see your inner star that is ready to shine.

This special edition of *The Image of Leadership for Sales* is particularly dear to my heart, as I grew up in sales during my corporate career. The majority of my professional journey took place at Europe's largest retail and tourism company.

Every day, every moment, every interaction, and every task was driven by one overarching objective: increasing sales. Even if you weren't in the sales department, such as my role leading the top management academy, every program, every training session, and every coaching initiative was designed to support the fundamental goal of increasing sales.

The experience of working in such sales-intensive environments has given me a profound understanding of the intricacies involved in the sales process. And while many say, "Everyone is in sales these days," and while this might be true, those who have deliberately chosen the sales path as their career know there are specific challenges and knowledge necessary when you breathe sales with every pore of your being. It's not just about closing deals; it's about creating value, building relationships, and understanding the unique needs of each client.

So let's get started on this exciting journey to achieving your full sales leadership potential.

Love,
Sylvie

Chapter 1
Seven Seconds

Seven Seconds:
Just a Glimpse, but the Vision Lasts.
1 2 **3 4 5 6 7**

Chapter 1: Seven Seconds

Appearance matters. Every hour of every day, we evaluate our environment based on what we see and hear. We avoid situations and individuals that seem threatening. Instead, we gravitate toward situations and individuals that appear welcoming. When we meet someone, we use sensory information to quickly determine if we're going to get along with them or if we need to keep our distance. We turn on the television and say, "This show looks good. I think I'll watch it." At the store, we inspect the food we want to buy. When a dog approaches us on the street, before we extend our hand, we examine its body language. Is the tail wagging, or is the dog tense? Just as we judge others, we're judged by the people who meet us and who simply see us. Do we appear trustworthy...confident...uncertain...detached? People we meet make quick decisions about us. Should they hire us, vote for us, buy something from us?

Research supports these concepts of quick judgment. Some studies suggest it takes from as few as milli seconds to as many as eleven seconds for people to delineate the various characteristics they use to judge us. In my professional work I've focused on the study that implies judgment occurs within seven seconds.
That study was conducted by psychologist Dr. Michael Solomon at NYU. It suggests our initial imprint is not based on a single element; instead, it is a composite of at least eleven elements that is subconsciously applied within those first seven seconds of meeting someone.

Here are those eleven elements:

- Socioeconomic level
- Education level
- Competence and honesty, believability, and perceived credibility
- Sex role identification
- Level of sophistication
- Trustworthiness
- Level of success
- Ethnicity
- Religious background
- Political background
- Social/sexual/professional desirability

Yet it's imperative to approach this list with a discerning mind. On one enlightening occasion I was honored to engage Dr. Solomon in conversation, and he shared a significant point with me: like many scientific findings, some interpretations of his study have been bent to fit various narratives across the internet and by self-proclaimed experts. It's one of those pervasive myths that human judgment rigidly conforms to his eleven-elements-and-seven-seconds rule. But his study never confirmed that hypothesis. In addition, his study is often taken out of context.

But the exact length of time and numbers of decisions don't really matter.

What does matter is that these judgments happen automatically in our brains, no matter whether we're aware of them, no matter whether we find them fair, and no matter whether, under our shabby clothes, we harbor the soul of Mother Teresa.

Before a client makes the decision to purchase a product or service from you, that client first needs to buy into you. The client needs to believe in your expertise, your integrity, and your ability to deliver on your promises. Your appearance is often the first step in building that trust.

Think about it this way: when clients meet you for the first time, they aren't just evaluating your product or your pitch. They are evaluating you as a person. They're asking themselves, "Is this someone I can trust? Is this someone who understands my needs? Is this someone who is professional, knowledgeable, and reliable?" Your appearance provides the first clues to answering those questions.

Of course, appearance alone isn't enough. You also need to have the substance to back it up. This means demonstrating your expertise, reliability, and value through various actions shown by your deep understanding of your products, services and industry; your ability to ask insightful questions and provide tailored solutions; your prompt and effective follow-up; and your commitment to exceeding client expectations.

It's about having a proven track record of success, being able to present compelling data and case studies, and being consistent in delivering on your promises. But in those crucial first moments, your appearance sets the stage for the relationship. It's the foundation upon which trust is built.

Anyone who aspires to a position of leadership in any capacity needs to understand the power of image. The good news is that your image of leadership is something you can control. You can make it what you want. It's a combination of how you appear, how you behave, how you communicate (online and offline), and how you operate within your environment. All of these are factors you can shape to work in your favor and that will help you rise to the level of leadership you desire.

Let's start with a story about two sales professionals, Michael and David, who are aiming for a key leadership position within a corporate setting. They're competing for the role of Vice President of Sales at a prestigious Fortune 500 company, a step that would represent a major advancement in their respective careers.

Although the story revolves around getting hired, the principles revealed in the story are true across any situation, whether sales professionals are seeking to elevate their client relationships, sales consultants are pitching to a major client, sales professionals are trying to book more qualified meetings, account executives are negotiating a major deal renewal, or sales engineers are demonstrating complex product capabilities.

First, let's meet Michael. Brimming with the anticipation of securing the role, he waits in the sleek lobby of the company's main building. Jennifer, the Chief Sales Officer, arrives to greet him. With a confident smile that's both friendly and businesslike, she shakes his hand with a firm grip before leading him toward her office.

As they walk through the open-concept office, passing clusters of focused team members and dynamic sales dashboards, there's a thoughtful yet uncomfortable silence between them. Upon arriving at her glass-walled office, Jennifer gestures for Michael to take a seat. She then moves to her side of the desk and, with a brief smile, she scans his résumé. Her questions are straightforward. Her inquiries are pointed. She delves into his sales successes and explores the distinctive sales skills he would bring to the team.

Michael feels uneasy. He doesn't think he's connecting with Jennifer. His credentials are solid—his résumé is what secured him this invitation—but he senses Jennifer is seeking something more—or something else. He feels the opportunity slipping away like water through his fingers. He can't pinpoint the issue. "Maybe," he speculates, "Jennifer is simply methodical and reserved by nature. After all, assessing sales professionals is part of her routine, and maybe she prefers to keep an objective stance, affording each candidate the same detached appraisal."

After twenty minutes, Jennifer closes Michael's file and looks up. "Well then, do you have any questions for me?" Michael has a multitude of questions, but Jennifer's composed conduct has thrown him off balance. He hesitates, then replies that he has no questions at the moment before inquiring about the next steps.

"As I'm sure you will understand," Jennifer says, "we have a significant number of candidates for this role. This initial interview is just the start of the process. We'll be in touch by next week. Thank you for coming in and for showing interest in the position."

She rises and shows Michael to the door. As Michael walks out of the sliding doors of the headquarters, he senses he's been hastily ushered out. His prospects for a callback, he thinks, are not good.

Now let's see how David does during the same process with a resume equal to Michael's.

Just as Michael did, David receives a warm reception from Jennifer in the lobby of the company's main building. Her smile is engaging, and with a confident handshake, she welcomes him before they walk toward her office. Throughout the brief walk they see teams engaged in their work with the soft hum of sales calls in the background. David and Jennifer initiate a light conversation.

"So how long have you been with this organization?" David asks.

"Did you have any trouble finding the place?" she asks, followed by an offer: "Would you like a water or coffee before we get started?"

When they reach her office, Jennifer gestures for David to take a seat while she settles into her own. With a sincere smile and a quick review of his résumé, it's clear that David's experience speaks for itself. Jennifer then delves into his professional background, asking what fresh perspectives he could bring to the sales team.

When David brings up a sales campaign that he heard Jennifer's company is launching, her interest is piqued, and she leans forward attentively, pressing him for details on his strategic approach. Sensing an opportunity to delve deeper, she wonders if he'd be open to discussing his ideas about this campaign with the Senior Sales Manager. David agrees without hesitation. A quick message is sent, and the senior sales manager soon joins them, giving David the chance to display his insight and proficiency directly.

An hour after David's arrival, Jennifer notes regretfully that she must excuse herself for another commitment but wonders if he is available to continue their conversation next week.

David confirms his availability and expresses his appreciation for the engaging discussion.

Stepping out of the company's offices, David feels a surge of confidence. He's established a meaningful rapport with both Jennifer, the Chief Sales Officer, and the Senior Sales Manager. And David feels optimistic about the next interview he has scheduled for later in the week with another major player in the industry, a fierce competitor of Jennifer's company.

At the executive leadership meeting the following day, Jennifer shares her insights about the candidates for the Vice President of Sales role. Michael's qualifications are considered first. "No," says Jennifer decisively. "He doesn't fit the bill. He lacked conviction. I can't picture him as part of our team." Then David's profile comes up. "Very impressive," remarks Jennifer. "He exudes leadership. He has an energetic presence. I believe if we brought him on board, he'd be impactful right out of the gate."

Michael and David, two capable sales professionals with equivalent qualifications yet, in the eyes of Jennifer, one seemed mismatched, the other distinguished.

If you were to ask Jennifer what made the difference between Michael and David, she might not say it was the way they presented themselves that set David well ahead of Michael. And, of course, many other factors were involved. But in the corporate world where a professional appearance can reflect an individual's meticulousness and diligence, their look might have played a crucial role.

Especially in a field such as sales that is characterized by persuasion, even if Michael had been dressed appropriately, it could have been his unadorned suit (lacking a hint of personal flair) or his conservative accessories (missing a spark of charisma) that didn't imprint upon Jennifer the image of a dynamic, compelling force beneath an unremarkable exterior.

She may not acknowledge that her opinion of Michael was formed from the moment she saw him in the company's lobby, dressed understated, seated leisurely, his posture a little too relaxed, his gaze idly locked on his smartphone, scarcely aware of the activity around him. His apparent lack of engagement with his surroundings might have inadvertently suggested an absence of the readiness or drive that is prized in the fast-moving world of corporate sales.

The interview? It might have been just an obligation, a formality. Michael may never have had a chance. As soon as she could, Jennifer ended the interview and showed him the door. Despite Michael's potential, he wasn't given a real chance.

In both recruitment and executive circles, the visual appearance and perception of a candidate or colleague is often an unspoken consideration. Although it may be regarded as trivial and go unacknowledged as part of the formal evaluation process, it still plays a part in decision-making.

Furthermore, legal and ethical standards prevent citing appearance as a reason for employment decisions. Jennifer couldn't and wouldn't explicitly say, "We can't bring you into our sales team because your personal appearance doesn't align with our expectations." Such a statement would cross professional boundaries and could lead to significant repercussions.

Jennifer also might not acknowledge that she had formed an opinion about the candidates before they even met, influenced by their credentials and images presented in their applications and online personas. Nonetheless, the reality is that, in any environment, the impression made by someone's appearance can subtly influence the final decision.

The principles illustrated in this story go well beyond just the job interview setting. They are also highly relevant in your interactions with prospects or clients across a variety of sales scenarios.

When you meet with a potential client to pitch a product or service, the way you present yourself can significantly influence the client's perception of your offering and their decision-making.

Similarly, during contract negotiations or deal renewals, your look of leadership and the way you command a room impacts how seriously the client takes your proposals and counteroffers.

Even in casual sales conversations and informal meetings, the impression you make shapes the client's overall experience and view of your capabilities. The concepts extend to sales presentations, product demos, trade shows, and any client-facing event. How confidently and dynamically you represent the organization and offering affects whether prospects or clients see you as a credible authority worth investing in.

While your skills, knowledge, and deliverables are paramount, the subtle yet powerful cues of your presence frequently influence a client's subconscious impressions of your expertise, diligence, and potential value. It shapes their openness to being influenced and guided by you through the buying journey.

A well-curated appearance sends a message of competence and dependability, establishing trust from the moment you step into a room. It's not just about looking good; it's about demonstrating respect for your role, the products or services you sell, the organization you work for, and the people you do business with.

It may be true that "you can't judge a book by its cover," but the hard reality is that, every day, in countless workplace interactions, sales professionals are judged by their "covers"—whether it's power suits in boardrooms, business casual in client meetings, statement accessories that add a touch of personality, meticulous grooming that highlights facial features, or even the style and condition of a pair of shoes.

Such judgments may not be fair, but they are the result of an intrinsic human instinct. Although we encourage looking beyond the surface, in many cases there isn't enough time to form opinions based on deep observation. That's why the brain defaults to the path of least resistance, the most straightforward route for gathering information—through our eyes. Humans are, after all, visual creatures.

Just imagine walking into a client's office for the first time to pitch your product or service. In those initial moments when you introduce yourself and get settled, you don't have much time to persuade with facts and figures.

That means the client's first impression is dictated primarily by how you carry yourself and your overall presence.

Or think about joining a video conference sales call. Before you even begin speaking, the client has already subconsciously evaluated your appearance, body language, facial expressions, and the setup behind you. Those visuals shape a client's perception before you can deliver your value proposition.

Even when sending prospecting emails or social media messages, any visual elements associated with your outreach contribute to whether a prospect sees you as someone credible and worth further engagement or not. Your email signature, the fonts you use in your emails, any emojis you add, the picture on your profile—each set the tone for your personal identity.

At trade shows or industry events, as others brush past your exhibit booth, it's the polish and charisma of your team's presence that first catches people's attention and establishes a sense of legitimacy.

While you aim to forge deeper connections over time, those opening seconds—guided by intrinsic visual biases—can make or break the initial impression, which then paves the path for genuine opportunities to demonstrate your expertise.

Research led by Doug Vogel at the University of Arizona illuminated the speed at which our brains process images—60,000 times faster than text—and found that 90 percent of information is transmitted visually.

Further emphasizing the predominance of visual information, Dr. Mary Potter from MIT led a study that found the human brain can process images in as little as thirteen milliseconds. This rapid processing suggests our brains are constantly and efficiently working to understand our visual world.

These astounding facts highlight the immediate impact of visual cues on our perception, and that impact makes your appearance a powerful communication tool.

Back at the interview, Michael might have believed his monochromatic attire was neutral enough to be acceptable based on his experience. But the moment Jennifer observed him, her internal judgment was clear-cut. She might have thought, "This candidate doesn't grasp the essence of our brand's identity. And I don't have time to teach him."

Of course, it's possible that in a different company, at another sales department, or for another sales leadership position Michael's attire and conduct would not have been pivotal factors. But for Jennifer's standards and the particular sales role Michael sought, they were.

And your prospects or clients might think something similar: This sales professional doesn't understand or align with our company culture and values. If this person can't represent himself properly, how can I trust him to represent us?

Your prospects or clients may subconsciously wonder if your lackluster first impression is indicative of the kind of mediocre experience they can expect when working with you and your organization. Fair or not, they make assumptions that your outward image directly correlates with your internal drive, expertise, and potential to deliver an outstanding result.

This principle, of course, also extends to your interactions as a leader with your sales team. As a sales leader your professional identity sets the tone for your team's professional standards. Team members look to you for cues on how to present themselves, how to behave in client interactions, and how to uphold the organization's values and culture. If you consistently present yourself with excellence, you inspire your team to do the same.

Conversely, if your professional identity is inconsistent or lacks excellence, it can undermine your authority and negatively impact team morale and performance. Your team may begin to question your commitment and capability, leading to a lack of respect.

By embodying the standards you expect from your team, you reinforce a culture of excellence and reliability, ensuring that your team members are motivated to mirror those qualities in their own roles.

Whether interacting with prospects, clients, or team members, the split-second visual analysis of whether this person embodies the qualities, professionalism, and commitment we're seeking can overrule other positive attributes you bring to the table. Your prospects may dismiss you before fully appreciating the value you could provide, simply because your initial visual cues didn't inspire their confidence.

A client may think, "This sales professional doesn't seem suited for the strategic partnership we're looking to build." Their lack of polish makes me question if they truly understand the complexities of our business. Or a client purchasing a premium offering may conclude that this sales professional's understated style doesn't match the prestigious image and top-tier experience they're seeking.

Conversely, a client with a more casual, start-up vibe may feel a highly formal, corporate sales professional seems stiff and out-of-touch with their innovative, fast-paced mentality.

Just as companies judge candidates, prospects and clients judge sales professionals through the lens of their own requirements and environments. The subtle cues of a sales professional's appearance and conduct are filtered through the client's perceptions of what an ideal partner should look and act like for their situation. A mismatch can lead to disqualification before dealing with core competencies.

Your goal is to reflect an understanding of the environment you wish to join and to show you can seamlessly integrate into the professional culture of the organization, whether it's during an interview, while pitching a product or service to a prospect, or negotiating with a client.

As for David, the moment Jennifer saw him—even before they shook hands—she knew he was a contender.

His outfit, the style of his hair, his choice of accessories, his impeccable shoes—all were indicative of a professional who viewed himself as a leader. And not just any leader, but one who could resonate with the dynamic spirit of a sales environment.

It might have been his creative flair in selecting clothes that broke the monotony, his unique way of marrying classic style with a modern twist, or his special knack for choosing accessories that hinted at a bold, strategic mind. We'll never know for certain. But something sparked the realization in Jennifer that "he gets it."

Yet, it wasn't vanity that dictated David's look. Far from being a glossy figurehead, his visual appearance stemmed from self-assurance. Standing tall, composed, and alert in the waiting area, he projected readiness and anticipation for the interview.

When Jennifer approached, David's smile was wide and authentic, generating a silent yet powerful first impression. He stepped forward, extending his hand first, ensuring a handshake that was confident and steady. Every micro-expression and gesture, from his steady eye contact to his assertive stance, communicated leadership.

Those subtle cues were the threads that wove a positive impression for Jennifer. David's outward presentation reflected his internal preparedness, a synchrony that Jennifer keenly observed. It was the finesse that transformed a prospect into a serious candidate.

David aimed to present himself as successful but, more critically, he wanted to be recognized as someone who could seamlessly integrate into the company's ethos. He hoped Jennifer would see past his attire and acknowledge his potential to meaningfully contribute. He aspired to render his appearance inconsequential, to be trusted immediately and seen as capable of excellence. David aimed to personify leadership, not through ostentation but through an aura of confidence that could galvanize a team to achieve new heights.

The Cost of a Poor Professional Imprint

Although it's your duty to maintain a positive professional identity, it's understood that perfection is unattainable and everyone, even those in the highest echelons of their field, is prone to missteps. Some errors may go unnoticed, but others could become widely known, perhaps through a viral social media post.

It could be a lapse in decorum at a company gala, an inadvertently shared comment that doesn't sit well publicly, or a day when your look of leadership might not meet the expected standards of your role. Not upholding the highest professional standards in every aspect of your work can result in significant consequences, such as the following:

- **Diminished credibility:** A sales professional's appearance may unfairly influence others' perceptions, potentially leading to a decrease in their perceived authority.

- **Loss of respect from team members or colleagues:** They may struggle to respect leaders who do not consistently present themselves at their best, affecting team dynamics and performance.

- **Distraction from leadership objectives:** A distracting appearance can draw attention away from a sales leader's strategic goals and the primary focus of driving organizational success.

- **Stagnant career trajectory:** Being viewed as unprofessional can hinder a sales professional's chances of promotion or landing larger, more lucrative accounts and territories.

- **Financial consequences:** Professionalism, or the lack thereof, can influence client retention and business outcomes, directly affecting the organization's bottom line.

- **Diminished earning potential:** A sales professional's perceived lack of professionalism can impact the ability to close deals and, hence, earn commissions or bonuses.

- **Public image risks:** A lapse in professionalism can quickly become amplified in the media, social media, or public forums, damaging your and your organization's reputation.

- **Undermining of professional boundaries:** Inappropriate attire can blur the lines of professional boundaries, increasing the risk of misinterpretation or misconduct.

While maintaining a positive professional identity is crucial for leaders within an organization, it is arguably even more vital for sales professionals whose roles are centered on client-facing activities and nurturing business relationships. Although perfection is an unrealistic standard, any lapses can severely undermine a sales professional's credibility and the organization's reputation in the eyes of prospects and clients. Not upholding the highest standards can result in significant consequences, such as:

- **Client mistrust:** A sales professional's questionable appearance can unfairly make prospects or clients doubt their expertise and question whether they can truly understand the client's needs.

- **Stalled negotiations:** Prospects may hesitate to enter deals or renew contracts with sales professionals who fail to consistently present a capable image aligned with the partnership value.

- **Opportunity cost:** A lack of professional polish can cause prospects to dismiss sales professionals before their skills are given a fair evaluation, resulting in missed revenue.

- **Weakened relationships:** Prospects and clients may limit future engagement if they believe the sales professional doesn't respectfully represent the standards expected of a strategic partner.

- **Competitive disadvantages:** If a sales professional's professionalism pales in comparison to competitors vying for the same opportunities, it can be an easy tiebreaker for prospects to dismiss them.

- **Lost revenue streams:** If key prospects or clients take their business elsewhere due to a sales professional's unprofessional conduct, it can mean huge revenue losses for the organization.

- **Pipeline erosion:** An unprofessional reputation can make it extremely difficult for a sales professional to refill their pipeline with quality prospects.

- **Department underperformance:** When one or more sales professionals aren't upholding professional standards, it can drag down the metrics and achievements of the entire sales team.

- **Impeded growth:** Company growth and expansion into new markets can be stunted if the sales team lacks the professionalism to be taken seriously.

You think this sounds far-fetched? Please think again.

Yes, when we reflect on the journey toward greater inclusivity in the professional world, we should recognize that overly rigid rules and stereotypes regarding personal appearance have significantly evolved. Gone are the days when draconian dress codes were stringently enforced without regard to individual expression.

Yet, there's still a pervasive trend to evaluate sales professionals on their aesthetic presentation on top of their skill set or personal attributes, even when appearance should hold no sway. But society often still appraises a sales professional's value through the lens of physicality.

And sales professionals themselves are not immune to internalizing such standards, often measuring their own worth by their reflection, which can ripple out and impact their confidence, focus, and overall performance in roles that have no bearing on looks. Navigating this tightrope of societal expectations can lead us to ask questions that resonate deeply with our struggle for identity in professional spaces. Here are some of those questions:

- Do I need to invest in luxury brands to create a successful professional identity?
- How casual is too casual for my client meetings?
- Should I embrace a style that allows my personality to shine through?
- How much should I be influenced by my organization's branding and culture?
- Do I need to adapt my style depending on the client's industry, size, or cultural norms?
- Should I make an effort to appear younger and more relatable to prospects or clients, or should I lean into a more mature, distinguished look?
- How do I strike the right balance between comfort and elevated presence for those countless hours in meetings or at tradeshows?
- Is there a risk of going too far with luxurious accessories and coming across as flashy rather than professional?

- Does it even matter when most of my sales calls are over the phone?
- How can I ensure my appearance isn't disheveled after hours of driving or flying?
- For those casual "grab-a-drink" prospect meetings, where is the line between being relatable and too lax?

Those are just a few of the underlying questions that cross many sales professionals' minds as they seek to balance the scales of authenticity and conformity with workplace norms.

Each choice is like a thread in the tapestry of our professional identity, woven together in hopes of crafting a presence that resonates with both who we are and who we aspire to be in our careers.

Are there easy answers to these questions?

No. There's no one-size-fits-all formula that can easily be applied for navigating these complexities, whether in person or online.

But the approach I advocate as you search for your answers is based on redirecting focus within those critical first seconds. The goal is to render your appearance neutral, ensuring it neither detracts from your goals nor defines you.

Instead, you want the spotlight on your expertise, your insights, and your contributions. It's about mastering the art of subtlety. Your aim should be that your presence—your eloquence, acumen, and ability—commands the room (or your social media feed), not what you're wearing.

When everything is about your experience, your added value, and your skills, your appearance becomes an inconsequential backdrop rather than the focal point. Strive to be memorable for your performance, not your style. And although this strategy applies to all roles, for sales professionals, achieving this may be a steeper climb because of the ongoing need for greater change in societal expectations and norms.

Ideally, your expertise should be the sole focus, but the nature of being in sales demands an exceptional ability to shape positive perception through your professional identity. The challenges you face in achieving this result are unique and include the following:

- **High-stakes first impressions:** In your line of work, those initial moments of meeting a prospect or client are critical for capturing their interest and establishing credibility. Fair or not, they make split-second judgments based on visual cues before you can fully demonstrate your expertise.

- **Perception is your product:** Unlike some other roles, your perceived professional identity is intrinsically tied to the perceived value of what you are selling. The "packaging" you present matters immensely.

- **Constantly being evaluated:** You are perpetually being sized up by prospects or clients who are looking for any reason, including your appearance, to disqualify you.

- **Representing the brand:** As the face of your organization, you are expected to visually and behaviorally embody the organization brand and values at all times.

- **Under observation 24/7:** Even when not in a typical sales situation, you are under observation, whether at community events, on vacations, or in other public settings. You are always perceived as a representative of your products, services, and organization's brand.

- **Overcoming preconceptions:** You must work harder to overcome any preexisting skepticism prospects may have that is based on your initial visible representation before you have opportunities to prove your capabilities.

- **Adaptability and resilience:** Sales professionals often face rejection and setbacks. The ability to quickly adapt to changing circumstances, stay resilient and maintain a positive attitude is vital for sustained success.

- **Emotionally driven environments:** When significant sums of money, their own personal health, or the well-being of their children are at stake, prospects or clients tend to be more emotionally driven. These heightened emotions can profoundly influence their decisions.

- **Cultural differences:** Rarely do sales professionals interact exclusively in a single cultural context. Their prospects and clients come from diverse cultural backgrounds, each with its own set of expectations, communication styles, and business etiquettes. This diversity necessitates a nuanced understanding and adaptability to navigate cross-cultural interactions.

- **Continuous learning:** The best sales professionals are committed to continuous learning and development. Staying updated with industry trends, improving skills, and seeking more knowledge are essential for staying competitive. With prospects and clients having unprecedented access to information, you must be prepared to engage with well-informed prospects or clients who expect a higher level of expertise and insight than ever.

- **Evolving competition:** The landscape of sales is rapidly changing with the continued evolution of the internet, artificial intelligence, augmented reality, and other technological advancements. These innovations shape client expectations and redefine the ways in which you must present yourself and your solutions.

And as we strive to achieve all of these objectives, it's imperative, again, to acknowledge that nobody is perfect. We all have off days. We all are humans. We aren't robots. We're not always going to be picture-perfect in those first few seconds. We're not always going to choose the right outfit, right attitude, right words. We can't understand everyone's mindset while scrolling through our social media feed. We're not always going to be confident, prepared, or able to do what's expected. But what we can do is always try our best and realize that an initial impression is just that—a beginning.

Chapter 2
Your Professional Imprint

The Indelible Mark
Etched in Others' Minds

Chapter 2:
Your Professional Imprint

L et's begin with some clarity on the lingo. Terms abound in the context of professional imprint. Some might refer to it as "executive presence" or "professional image." Others might use "professional identity," and there are those who speak of "personal branding." Each term, although distinct, converges on a core principle: the essence of how you present, position, and define yourself in your career.

Yet it's the initial interaction, this "professional imprint," that etches your reputation into the minds of others during those initial fleeting moments when the ephemeral dance of first impressions sets the stage for the enduring narrative of your professional saga. But this professional imprint is more than just a first impression; it's the genesis of your reputation, the spark that ignites the perception of your professional identity and professional brand in the workplace.

Our professional imprint is a direct reflection of the attention and care we invest in our most valuable asset—ourselves. It's evident in the meticulous choices we make, from the polished shoes that carry us through our endeavors to the precision with which we tailor our clothing, ensuring every line contributes to a professional identity of competence and confidence. It's the thoughtful selection of a workbag, not merely as a container but as a symbol of readiness for whatever the day may bring. Take, for example, the care we exercise in choosing eyewear, which not only sharpens our vision but also frames our intent and focus.

Each decision, each deliberate act of presentation, weaves together the rich tapestry that becomes our visual narrative, inviting observers to read competence and readiness into our appearance.

Each detail is a thread in the fabric of the impression we weave, not only benefitting our self-image but enhancing the esteem of the organizations we represent.

Because the reputation of any organization—whether it's a corporate entity, entrepreneurial venture, educational or government organization, or nonprofit—is significantly influenced by the appearance and conduct of its representatives. This is particularly true for sales professionals. As the direct link between the organization and its prospects or clients, they are often the first point of contact and play a crucial role in shaping client perceptions. Their professional identity can either reinforce the organization's credibility or undermine it, making their conduct pivotal in establishing and maintaining a positive reputation.

In every industry, from private firms to public service, individuals reflect not just their personal identity but also the ethos of their employer. Whether in a bustling corporate office or a dynamic start-up, every individual, from the front desk to the executive suite, must offer stakeholders the best possible reflection of their professional commitment. After all, employees are the living embodiment of any organization's values and principles.

So it's imperative that sales professionals' first interactions, whether with prospects, clients, or business partners, set a tone. It's in those first moments that their appearance becomes pivotal. It's the first tangible demonstration of their adherence to excellence and their pledge to uphold the organization's standards.

Although the story of Michael and David unfolded in a corporate environment, the essence of the so-called seven-second rule is universal. Whether you're stepping into a high-stakes client meeting, engaging in a virtual sales conference, posting updates on social media, presenting a business proposal, or attending a networking event, your professional imprint is established almost instantly.

Changing this first imprint once it's formed is notoriously difficult because first impressions are anchored in the primal corners of our brain where quick judgments were once necessary for survival. These initial categorizations, often made subconsciously, are our mind's rapid response to new stimuli, and once they are formed, they become a filter through which all subsequent interactions are assessed.

For example, when Jennifer initially encountered Michael and unconsciously placed him in the "not suitable" category, changing that snap judgment was nearly impossible. It was rooted in Jennifer's cognitive framework that subconsciously forced her to seek information that would reinforce her initial perception while ignoring evidence to the contrary. Michael's chance to make a positive impression was lost before it began.

On the flip side, when Jennifer met David, his professional presentation immediately pegged him as credible and competent. Jennifer's swift categorization was governed by the same cognitive processes that shaped her earlier judgment. Subconsciously, her brain was compelled to confirm her initial favorable impression, scanning for evidence to support David's suitability. In this subtle dance of cognition, her brain worked diligently, albeit unknowingly, to validate that David was, indeed, the exemplary choice for the role at hand.

This is the power of a professional imprint. It is the ambition of every professional—particularly sales leaders who often face more nuanced challenges than others in this regard—to be seen instantly as competent and capable, maximizing every opportunity to exhibit leadership potential.

Those critical moments of assessment can happen in any professional environment. Michael might have been a sales consultant discussing a business strategy, or David could have been an entrepreneur pitching his start-up vision. The context may vary, but the specific situation matters less than this universal truth: within those first crucial seconds, based on their self-presentation, people are categorized as "doubtful" or "promising."

For those first moments I'm not talking about your DNA. It's not about how tall you are or your body type, although those factors do play a role, as you will find out later in this book. I'm talking about the countless things you can control—regardless of the qualities bestowed upon you by the vagaries of the genetic lottery—to develop your best qualities (we all have them) and minimize your liabilities (we all have those too).

Additionally, your look of leadership shapes not only how you're perceived by others but also how you perceive yourself. Looking the part can significantly enhance your confidence and effectiveness. For sales professionals in various environments this means choosing clothing that projects confidence, competence, and authenticity, whether you're in the boardroom, participating in a networking event, or conducting virtual meetings. It's about finding that balance between professional standards and personal style that allows you to feel authentic and act with authority.

It's not a matter of wearing power suits every day or specialized clothing; it's a matter of finding the proper balance where you feel empowered and can broadcast your professional best.

The clothing choices we make can act as a form of self-expression, offering a visual language that communicates our identity, mood, and confidence level—not just to others but to ourselves. When sales professionals wear clothes that align with their role and that they feel good in, it can create a positive feedback loop: they may feel more confident and in control, and that can elevate their sales performance and the quality of their client interactions.

For many sales leaders, the right outfit serves as armor against the world, providing a sense of preparedness for whatever the day may bring. It can also signal to others that they take their role seriously and command respect. There's a reason terms like "power dressing" have emerged; clothing can be empowering.

Research by Hajo Adam and Adam D. Galinsky from Northwestern University has shown that, when you dress in a way that you perceive as powerful, you can experience psychological changes that include increased abstract thinking, which is a key component of leadership and strategic thought.

This intersection of clothing and psychology is known as "enclothed cognition," which describes the impact clothes have on the wearer's psychological processes. Enclothed cognition is a powerful testament to how the external—the clothes we choose and the professional identity we present—intersects with the internal, shaping how we see ourselves and, in turn, how we are perceived as leaders.

Therefore, it's no wonder this concept becomes pivotal in the microseconds during which we make an entrance, be it in a physical room or a virtual meeting space. In these first micro-moments, our visual appearance leaves a swift yet indelible mark, informing others' instantaneous judgments about our capabilities. This initial imprint, a snapshot taken by the observer's mind, sets the stage for all subsequent interactions and opportunities.

Imprinting can be demonstrated easily. When I speak at an event, I usually enter the stage and count out loud to seven, demonstrating how fleeting yet critical this moment is for setting the tone of the audience's perception. Then I open the plethora of decisions audience members have already made about me without knowing anything about my background, skills, knowledge, or the value I bring to the event.

Let's look back at Jennifer for an example. While assessing potential team members, certain elements such as sex role identification, ethnicity, religious and political background, and sexual desirability should not influence her judgment and are ethically and legally required to hold no sway in professional evaluations.

But attributes such as competence, honesty, believability, credibility, and trustworthiness are paramount. Jennifer's initial assessment of Michael's and David's presentations probably led her to subconsciously categorize them based on critical professional qualities.

In contrast, when prospects or clients interact with you, some of those eleven elements take on heightened importance in driving perception. Elements like your socioeconomic level and education background can signal your ability to understand and speak to their world as a colleague. Your level of sophistication conveys whether you can navigate their cultural norms with polish. Perceived competence and credibility are paramount for instilling confidence that you grasp their complex needs. Your trustworthiness and perceived honesty remain crucial drivers for prospects and clients. Both are vetting whether you have grasped their challenges and can be a transparent, ethical partner. Your projected level of success—the presence that you are a proven winner who can drive results for them—is a pivotal factor in those opening moments.

As a sales leader within your organization, one who is responsible for inspiring and guiding your sales team, many of those eleven elements take on a distinct significance in how you are perceived and evaluated by colleagues, upper management, and your team members.

Competence, credibility, and trustworthiness remain paramount for you as a sales leader, just as with client interactions. Your team needs to perceive you as a skilled authority who can be trusted to provide guidance and ethical leadership.

But elements like your socioeconomic status and education may take a back seat after you establish a successful track record within the organization.

Your level of sophistication also remains important, but more so in how it allows you to embody the organizational culture, values, and professional expectations in representing the organization's brand.

While aspects like your ethnicity, religion, politics, or sex role identification should still be nonfactors, traits like your honesty, believability, and perceived ethics come under heightened scrutiny. Your team needs to buy into you as a leader who upholds uncompromising integrity.

While the eleven elements remain consistent, their weightings shift based on the observer's motives. Although we might hope these initial imprints could evolve, most of us know how challenging it can be to reshape first opinions. Those impressions are the lens through which all subsequent qualities are filtered, and not acknowledging these early signals can lead to difficulties.

The Science of First Impressions

Let me introduce you to one more study on the subject of first impressions. We'll take a close look at how this research was carried out, dissecting each step of the study to fully understand the results and their implications for our daily interactions. But it's important to remember that this is only a single piece of a larger scientific consensus and cannot be universally applied to every situation precisely as described. It's a reflection of a broad scientific understanding that, even though first impressions can be powerful and enduring, specific outcomes and interpretations may vary depending on context and individual circumstances.

Neuroscientists at NYU and Harvard identified the neural systems involved in forming first impressions. Their study, which shows how we encode social information and then evaluate it in making initial judgments, was conducted in the laboratory of Elizabeth Phelps and reported in the journal *Nature Neuroscience*.

The study was based on the concept that each new person we meet presents a set of ambiguous and complex information. Because it's a first meeting, the information is primarily visual, although other senses—hearing, smell, and even touch (if you shake hands, e.g.)—can come into play.

We quickly sort through this information and judge whether we're attracted to that person or not. It's an ancient and deeply embedded process that allowed our ancestors to quickly assess their relationship to a new person—friend or foe, social superior or inferior? And perhaps most significantly, will this person be useful to the group—a leader—or will the person be a burden?

But how does this complex process happen? The study sought to investigate the brain mechanisms that give rise to impressions formed immediately after meeting a new person.

To explore the process of first impression formation, the researchers designed an experiment in which they examined brain activity when participants made initial evaluations of fictional individuals. The researchers gave participants written profiles of twenty individuals with a variety of personality traits. The profiles, presented alongside pictures of the fictional individuals, included scenarios indicating traits both positive (e.g., intelligent) and negative (e.g., lazy).

After reading the profiles, the participants were asked to evaluate how much they liked or disliked each profiled individual. The impressions varied depending on how much each participant valued the particular positive and negative traits conveyed. For instance, if a participant liked intelligence in a leader more than they disliked laziness, they might form a positive impression of that person.

During this impression formation period the researchers observed the brain activity of the participants by using functional magnetic resonance imaging (fMRI). Based on the participants' responses, the researchers measured the difference in brain activity when the participants encountered information that was more important in forming their first impressions.

During the encoding of impression-relevant information, the neuroimaging results revealed significant activity in two regions of the brain. The first, the posterior cingulate cortex, has been linked to making economic decisions and assigning subjective value to rewards.

The second, the amygdala, is a small structure in the medial temporal lobe that was previously linked to emotional learning about inanimate objects and social evaluations based on trust or racial group. Those parts of the brain showed increased activity when encoding information that was consistent with the impression.

The study also suggested that when we only briefly encounter others and have limited and ambiguous cues to evaluate, brain regions that are important in emotional learning and value representation are engaged. When encoding everyday social information during a social encounter, these regions sort information based on its personal and subjective significance and summarize it into a single value—a first initial imprint. Thus, we can formulate the following equation: our emotional learning + our values = the professional's imprint.

And this imprint is multidimensional, extending its influence far beyond the initial point of contact. It's an intricate interplay of personal and professional signals that collectively shape the narrative of our professional identity.

It's not a static or isolated occurrence; it's a dynamic force that echoes across various facets of our professional landscape. It's the subtle yet powerful undercurrent that can sway decisions, alter interactions, and steer the course of our professional journeys.

As we unpack the significance of this imprint, let's explore how it reverberates.

Consider the impact on you. When you, as a sales leader, project confidence and competence through your professional identity, you're more likely to feel empowered and capable in your role. This self-assurance can translate directly into improved sales performance and sales effectiveness.

Reflect on your familial and social circle. The way you present yourself professionally not only influences your own psyche, it extends to the perceptions of your family members, friends, and broader social networks. Upholding a professional identity can establish a halo of trust and respect that permeates your entire personal support system.

Think about those you interact with. Prospects or clients, colleagues or business partners—any professional stakeholders form their initial impressions of you based on various factors, including your appearance. By consciously presenting yourself in the best possible way, you inspire trust, credibility, and lay the groundwork for stronger business relationships and better outcomes.

Recognize the impact on your client's reputation. Your professional presentation doesn't just reflect on you, it significantly influences your client's reputation as well. Prospects or clients aspire to confidently say, "I work with [Your Company]," as a badge of credibility and prestige. When you represent yourself with excellence, you not only gain their trust, you empower them to leverage your association to enhance their own standing in the industry by reinforcing their own brand's integrity and professional identity.

Consider the impact on your team members. As a sales leader, the way you present yourself sets the tone and example for your entire sales team. Your professional identity provides team members with a model to emulate as they interact with prospects or clients. Strong leaders can inspire their team members to raise their own professional standards and assert a sense of pride and assurance in saying, "I'm led by [Your Name]."

Acknowledge the organization you represent. Whether operating within a corporate sales team, spearheading your own entrepreneurial sales endeavors, or collaborating with other sales professionals, the way you uphold high standards casts a reflection not just on you but on the organization(s) you're affiliated with. By embodying professionalism and integrity, you bolster your own professional identity as well as that of the collective entities you represent.

Think about future employers or partners. The professional identity you build through your consistent professionalism has a lasting impact. It can open doors for career opportunities, investments, or strategic partnerships by preceding you with a respected, credible image before you even meet potential employers or business partners.

Reflect on the profession as a whole. Beyond just your current organization, the cumulative impact of sales professionals upholding the highest levels of excellence elevates societal perceptions of the sales profession overall. Your individual efforts contribute to greater respect and appreciation for the expertise, ethics, and values that elite sales leadership provides across all industries.

Evaluate the industry-wide implications. Your individual actions as a sales professional contribute to the collective image and societal perceptions of the sales industry as a whole and across all industries. Consistent displays of expertise and sophisticated presence can elevate public confidence in the value of sales leaders, encouraging a greater embrace of sales-driven businesses, initiatives, and authority.

Consider generational impact and legacy. The example you set helps shape the expectations and aspirations of the next generation of sales professionals. Your professional identity provides a benchmark for aspiring sales leaders to continuously raise the professional bar.

Therefore, it's essential to be mindful of how you present yourself in every interaction because it can have far-reaching effects. Whether you're engaging with prospects or clients, collaborating with colleagues, or representing your organization at industry events, your professional imprint extends beyond the immediate interaction.

As a sales leader, you are a beacon that illuminates the path for others in your field. The way you embody leadership sets a standard that reverberates through your team, your organization, and your industry. It's a powerful reminder that every interaction, every first impression, is an opportunity to elevate not just your own professional standing but the collective image of sales professionals everywhere.

So as you navigate the complex landscape of sales leadership, remember that your professional imprint is a reflection of the values, the expertise, and the integrity that define the essence of what it means to be a leader in sales. Embrace this responsibility with a keen awareness of the far-reaching impact of your actions and appearance, and you'll not only excel in your own career but contribute to the advancement of the entire sales profession.

The Sustained Imprint

Your initial impression is pivotal, yet it's merely the precursor to what must become a deeply rooted perception. Consider this the inception of your "sustained imprint." It's the ongoing cultivation of this first impression that cements your professional identity and maintains its potency. Without nurturing, even the most stellar beginnings can fade, losing their resonance and diminishing their initial influence. Your first imprint is only the beginning. Your sustained imprint needs to evolve into a lasting and positive impression.

I once organized a leadership seminar for a group of sales leaders from the retail and e-commerce company I worked for. The participants were surprised to find their trainers were not people but horses.

In one of the first exercises, we split the participants into two groups. The first group went into the riding area where an unleashed horse was waiting. The participants were told to walk straight in with confident steps, to appear strong, to maintain eye contact with the horse, and to keep a straight face.

When they arrived at the horse they were to smack their whips on the ground several times. When they did so, the horse immediately began to run in a circle. The participants continued to snap their whips, and they were briefed to stop when the horse appeared to tire or seemed ready for the next step.

When the participants put their whips aside, something magical happened: the horse followed them everywhere, yet none of the participants had said one word to the horse.

The second group received a different briefing. They were supposed to walk in and appear friendly and kind to the horse. They were told to motivate the horse by petting it, talking to it, and developing a relationship. They even brought in treats.

But that second group had a difficult time trying to make the horse run in a circle. It was obvious the horse wanted more treats and more tender loving care. The horse didn't follow the members of the second group, and it finally didn't even come back to see if there were more treats.

What did we learn? Horses, much like humans, respond to the nonverbal cues of confidence and assertiveness. The first group's authoritative approach, conveyed through their posture, gaze, and decisive actions, left a compelling imprint on the horse. The first group commanded respect and prompted a clear behavioral response. That experience underscored the power of a strong initial imprint; without uttering a single word, the first group's commanding conduct set the tone for the interaction, resulting in the horse's compliance and subsequent allegiance.

We also learned that being liked should not be the ultimate goal of leadership—being respected should be. As a leader, it's crucial to understand that respect is the foundation upon which effective leadership is built. Being liked is a bonus.

But this example doesn't mean you should start wielding a metaphorical whip in your leadership style or with your team members. Leadership is not about instilling fear or intimidation. It's about inspiring others through your actions and your unwavering commitment to excellence.

It's about creating a culture of mutual respect where everyone is encouraged to bring their best selves to the table and work toward a common goal. Leadership is not about force, it's about influence.

Throughout the next days at the seminar we also observed that the first group, emboldened by their initial success, celebrated their triumph, embodying the spirit of leadership and victory. But as time progressed, the complexity of their challenge unfolded. They began to display inconsistency in their conduct and actions. To the horse, their once clear and commanding presence became unpredictable. And predictability, consistency, form the cornerstone of leadership—it's what engenders trust and respect. We seek reliability in leaders' appearances, words, and decisions as well as in the steadiness of their conduct.

The first group, although initially successful in commanding attention, failed to uphold the robustness of that initial imprint. They did not succeed in cultivating it into a sustained imprint. The horse's diminishing responses were a clear testament to the group's faltering consistency. The lesson was vivid: a leader's impact is measured not only by the strength of the initial imprint but also by the ability to sustain it. The game isn't over after seven seconds. Outstanding sales leaders leave lasting impressions by how they consistently present themselves, always and everywhere.

Like David's experience, the positive imprint that developed in mere seconds only got him in the door. It made the possibility of acceptance real. It broke down the barrier between him and Jennifer. But the true test of his leadership and his professional identity will be in whether he can sustain and build upon that initial approval, confirming his value and substance in every subsequent interaction and decision. Conversely, the negative impression that Michael created caused the door to slam shut. It reduced the possibility of acceptance and created a barrier between him and the person he met who, in this case, had the power to either help him up the ladder of success or pass him by in favor of someone else.

He will never get the chance to prove his excellence or reveal the depth of his expertise because the brief encounter in the waiting area cast a shadow on his interview.

In the glass-walled high rises of corporate powerhouses or the energetic buzz of start-up hubs, whether navigating the structured pathways of B2B environments or the collaborative networks of B2C circles—even within the mission-driven walls of social enterprises—your initial imprint needs to be confirmed every day.

In every setting that calls for your close attention, every interaction and choice contributes to your lasting professional legacy. The warmth of a greeting, the thoughtfulness of an environment, and the focused attention offered to prospects or clients and colleagues alike are threads in the tapestry of your enduring reputation. Even outside the confines of your office, your influence extends into the community, whether at industry events or during casual interactions—even during moments you pay little attention to because, most of the day, you run on autopilot. And, like many of us, you fail to recognize that you're under constant observation.

I illustrate this reality in my keynotes by asking participants to take a selfie. As they excitedly prepare to capture their picture-perfect portrait, employing what digital culture has taught us—to position face and body perfectly, to smile, to raise an eyebrow—I interrupt them with a seemingly impossible challenge: no posing, no adjusting their hair, no straightening their posture, no putting on their best camera-ready face. No tilting the head to find the most flattering angle, no sucking in the stomach or pushing out the chest, no last-minute adjustments to clothing or accessories. Just take a raw, unfiltered snapshot of their authentic selves at that exact moment.

The result is a revelation, a picture that showcases how, most of the day, they are observed when they forget about their environments, when they forget they are always on stage, when they think no one is watching.

It's a stark contrast to the carefully curated images we often present to the world, a reminder that our true selves are not always the polished versions we'd like to think they are. That simple exercise is a powerful testament to the fact that our professional imprint is not just crafted in the moments we are acutely aware of but in the everyday instances when we let our guard down. It's in those instances that our authentic selves shine through, and it's those glimpses that can leave the most lasting impressions.

You might question whether the continuity of this positive, sustained imprint is solely contingent upon our appearance. Clearly, it's not the sole factor, yet it's significant. Your appearance, throughout the entire process, acts as a critical filter through which all your professional behaviors and communications are perceived. It's a silent but powerful language that precedes and punctuates every action. It sets the stage upon which your competencies are judged. Although not the entire story, it's an essential chapter in the narrative of your professional identity.

There's a famous study by Albert Mehrabian that suggests the words you say—the actual words, not the tone or inflection—account for only 7 percent of the imprint you make. It's called the "7-38-55 rule." Words account for 7 percent, tone of voice accounts for 38 percent, and body language accounts for 55 percent of the imprint you make.

You might think (or might have heard) that this study suggests it's not important what you say or how you behave; it's only about appearance. Of course, that's not true. It's another internet myth, and Mehrabian himself has made countless attempts to clarify that the study should not be interpreted that way.

Still, countless coaches, trainers, and speakers use this study to suggest the thing that matters most is how you appear, neglecting the significance of verbal communication and behavior.

But if you have only seven seconds to make an excellent first impression, your appearance takes on greater importance. In those fleeting moments, it's unlikely there will be time to showcase your behavior and communication skills.

Think of the countless times you've been in a client meeting and someone enters the room. Whether they're poised or disheveled, you instantly form an opinion. Or consider seeing someone at a networking event; their attire, from suits to casual wear, elicits immediate assumptions about their role or status. Picture yourself scrolling through your LinkedIn feed and pausing at a striking new profile picture that a colleague has posted. Or imagine that moment you walk into a potential client's office and the receptionist's elegant attire persuasively suggest the quality of the company's services before you've even met with the decision-maker. Each day, from a client's briefcase that catches your eye in a meeting, hinting at their taste, to observing a fellow attendee's book at a sales conference, silently inferring their interests and, perhaps, even their personality, we form impressions incessantly. These instances underscore a truth we all navigate—appearance often speaks first, and our brains are intricately wired to listen.

No one is exempt from this instinctive process; it is a fundamental aspect of our human cognition.

You'll recall that Michael and David had almost identical résumés. (This is not just a hypothetical; in today's competitive job marketplace, among dozens of qualified applicants for a given position there are bound to be several candidates who look virtually the same on paper.)

When Michael and David first met Jennifer, they probably said about the same thing. But those initial moments are too fleeting to demonstrate verbal competence. Instead, in such brief encounters it's our visual and, perhaps, even our sensed presence that speaks volumes. The human brain, in its quest for instant understanding, relies primarily on visual cues complemented by the subtle undercurrents of what it feels rather than what it hears.

As Michael and David awaited their turns to interview, silent narratives unfolded within moments of Jennifer's approach. They cast a long and, sometimes, indelible shadow, setting a stage for unseen forces to come into play. Those forces, subtly yet powerfully influenced the trajectory of Jennifer's judgments.

Like invisible threads, they pulled at the fabric of perception, weaving conclusions based on the initial visual encounter. Those energies, silent but potent, placed David in a halo of positive light but shrouded Michael in a cloud of skepticism.

For you, navigating this landscape with awareness and finesse can turn the tide of initial imprints and unconscious judgments in your favor, cementing a reputation that is resilient and sustainable. By honing your look of leadership and ensuring it aligns with your values, expertise, and organizational culture, you're not just dressing for success, you're embodying it.

Remember, your appearance is not about vanity, it's about strategy. It's a powerful nonverbal communicator that can open doors, command respect, and inspire trust. In a world where first impressions often become lasting ones, your appearance is your silent partner, working tirelessly to establish your credibility and reinforce your leadership.

The Invisible Filters of Perception

Put yourself in the shoes of a patient for just a moment. You find yourself needing quick medical care, and as you enter a doctor's practice, a sea of expectations and anxieties floods your mind. The receptionist is busy typing and fails to notice you right away. As seconds tick by—seconds that feel like an eternity—you start to feel ignored.

During that time your eyes wander, and you can't help but notice the receptionist's nails look like they could use some attention. Their makeup and hair seem a bit much for such an early hour. When they finally do greet you, your patience has worn thin. You were on time, but you were left waiting. Finally, while sitting in the waiting room you spot a crumpled piece of paper under a chair and notice that all the chairs show signs of age. Then, as you're called to see the doctor, a strange smell drifts from the staff room. "Maybe they just had lunch..."

The doctor comes to get you, moving quickly, not stopping for introductions or handshakes. The doctor's shoes have seen better days, and the white coat has lost some of its brightness. All those little things add up in your mind, painting a picture of a place that might not be up to the mark. "No wonder I was ignored, you think. This whole practice seems subpar."

What you just experienced is the powerful influence of unconscious biases, leading your mind to make snap judgments. The sights and impressions, from the receptionist's appearance to the subtle cues of the environment, all funnel through your perceptions, coloring your expectations, even if not a single word was spoken.

Let me share a personal anecdote that also illuminates how a variety of biases can work against us, even in the most intimate of settings. I am married to a German mathematician and engineer who works in finance and IT, so let's indulge in a few stereotypes about Germans. My husband requires that everything be sorted and organized in a particular way. He thrives on order and structure. My cultural background, on the other hand, is Mediterranean, which comes with a relaxed approach that embraces life's fullness and that finds joy in daily adventures that aren't always structured or planned.

I'm the wife who goes to the refrigerator, takes out a bottle of sparkling water, and puts it back without securing the cap as tightly as my German husband would expect. That behavior often leads to one of those minor household arguments that occur in most relationships. But here's the interesting part—he finds every single item I leave open, and I mean *every thing*. But he never seems to recognize the things I close, and I do close things.

What's at play here is a medley of biases working against me. His brain embarks on a journey that subconsciously seeks evidence to support his particular perception of me. He might think, "She's always leaving things open," or "She's not as organized as I am." But the reality is far more nuanced.

It's not that I never close things; it's just that his mind is attuned to noticing the instances that confirm his preconceived notions.

The same is true for your team members and prospects or clients. Their minds go on journeys too, shaping their perceptions based on a complex interplay of biases and preconceptions. They might fixate on a single interaction or characteristic that confirms their existing beliefs while overlooking the multitude of instances that contradict it.

As a sales leader, recognizing and navigating these biases is crucial. It's not about striving for perfection or trying to control every perception. Rather, it's about understanding that these biases exist and consistently presenting your authentic, best self in a way that invites others to see beyond their initial assumptions. It's about building a sustained imprint that, over time, paints a comprehensive picture of your leadership, one that acknowledges your unique strengths and style while demonstrating your adaptability and growth.

So the next time you find yourself in a situation where biases might be at play, remember my sparkling water story. Recognize that perceptions are often shaped by selective attention and confirmation bias. But also know that by consistently showing up as your authentic, best self, you have the power to gradually reshape those perceptions. Just as I continue to work on finding a balance between my relaxed approach and my husband's love for order, you can find ways to bridge the gap between others' assumptions and your true leadership potential.

For you as a sales leader, those same unconscious biases could come into play when your team interacts with you. Imagine one of your team members arriving for a critical meeting. If your office or meeting space appears disorganized with papers strewn about and unkempt surfaces, it could unintentionally signal a lack of professionalism or preparedness on your part. Your team may start questioning your attention to detail before you even begin the discussion.

Or if you greet your team members looking flustered, disheveled, or displaying poor grooming, their unconscious minds may jump to judgments about your ability to stay composed under pressure or properly represent the team's high standards when engaging with prospects or clients and executives.

Those snap impressions take on even higher stakes when sales leaders are interacting with prospects or clients. Envision walking into an important meeting. If the boardroom chairs appear worn and tattered, or there are distracting odors from an unkempt break room nearby, their unconscious biases may lead them to immediately doubt your organization's competence or commitment to quality before your pitch even begins.

Similarly, if you enter looking frazzled, those first unconscious judgments could tank their confidence in your capabilities and expertise. Those silent cues of disorganization and sloppiness can overpower even the most persuasive words and undermine your credibility.

The impactful takeaway is that we all innately make subconscious assessments that are further influenced by our unconscious biases. These biases are silent storytellers, weaving narratives that may not be accurate or fair, but they can shape interactions and decisions in profound ways.

These biases often stem from deeply embedded social stereotypes, personal experiences, or prevailing cultural norms.

Confirmation bias: This is one of the most prominent unconscious biases. Confirmation bias is a psychological phenomenon in which individuals favor information that confirms their preexisting beliefs or hypotheses. It's the tendency to seek information that validates their existing perceptions. This means we're more likely to notice details that support what we already think, often overlooking evidence to the contrary.

From the moment you walked through the door of that doctor's practice, your brain was picking up on cues and details that began to form an impression.

When the receptionist didn't immediately look up, their unpolished appearance confirmed any lurking thoughts that the practice might be disorganized or unprofessional. Each subsequent observation, from the crumpled paper to the worn furniture to the doctor's hurried entrance, built upon that initial judgment.

Instead of seeing those elements as isolated instances, confirmation bias led you to interpret them as part of a pattern, reinforcing the belief that the practice did not meet the standards you expected. Each detail seemed to confirm your initial impression; such bias can be challenging to overcome once it takes root.

Anchoring bias: This is another pervasive mental shortcut we often take when we rely too heavily on the first piece of information we receive—the anchor—and allow it to disproportionately influence our subsequent judgments and decisions. Once an anchor is set, other interpretations and information, even if more relevant or factual, tend to be viewed through the lens of this initial reference point.

Suppose the initial delay and the receptionist's disheveled appearance were the first bits of information you registered. Those details likely became your anchor. As you continued to wait, even before noticing the crumpled paper or the smell from the staff room, your mind was already anchored to the notion that this practice was subpar. This early anchor had an impact on your entire perception of the care provided, regardless of the actual quality of the medical services you received.

The horn effect: This leads you to attribute negative characteristics based on a single perceived flaw and causes you to view all traits of an individual or entity negatively. For example, the receptionist's posture, which could be neutral or simply a product of a long day, might seem to you to indicate a lack of interest or enthusiasm. This bias can lead you to overlook any instances of competence or moments of kindness, focusing instead on those traits that seem to confirm your initial negative impression.

Negativity bias: This is another cognitive phenomenon in which negative aspects have a more significant impact on an individual's psychological state than do neutral or positive aspects. Essentially, we tend to pay more attention to, and give more weight to, negative experiences or information.

Did you even notice the receptionist's meticulous uniform? Or what about the effort they put into carefully documenting patient cases, a sign of thoroughness and dedication? Did you observe the efficiency with which they eventually handled your paperwork or the accuracy of their data entry? Similarly, the doctor's speed may have been a reflection of the ability to manage a busy practice effectively, ensuring every patient receives timely care. But those positive traits may have been eclipsed by the more immediate negative judgments, steering your overall impression toward the unfavorable due to negativity bias.

Selection bias: This will further force your mind to focus on every little flaw. You notice the tiniest speck of dirt, a slight tear in the curtain, or a faint noise from the air conditioner. You continue to selectively focus on all the negatives while ignoring anything positive about the experience.

Self-serving bias: This might come into play when you think, *I always pick the wrong practice*, making you feel even more justified in your negative assessment. This bias reinforces the idea that the problem lies with the practice, not with any external factors or mere chance.

The illusion of control: This will make you feel like you could have avoided this bad experience if only you had chosen a different practice. You think you had control over the situation, and this misplaced belief adds to your frustration. And even after you've left the practice, unconscious biases continue to steer your mind.

Availability bias: This, for example, ensures you overestimate the likelihood or importance of certain events or outcomes based on their ease of recall or availability in memory. This means the negative aspects you noticed loom larger in your memory than the positive ones. The negative aspects are the examples that come to mind when you reflect on your visit.

This tendency can extend to the point where you might find yourself at home, browsing online reviews of the practice, unconsciously searching for confirmation of your initial opinion. As you skim through numerous positive testimonials, they barely register; instead, your attention zeroes in on the few critical remarks. Those resonate with your experience, reinforcing your perspective. Feeling validated, you consider it almost a duty to add your own critique.

The bandwagon effect: This is a bias that compels us to adopt beliefs or behaviors because they seem popular. In this context, the critical comments of others echo your own impressions, and the weight of collective criticism may feel like undeniable proof, further solidifying your initial judgments.

The Dunning–Kruger effect: This also may take hold as you consider leaving a review. Feeling qualified to evaluate the entire medical staff after a single visit, this bias overstates your own expertise, leading you to assert judgments that might not reflect the true caliber of the healthcare professionals' skills and services.

The sunk cost fallacy: This may cause you to persist in viewing the practice negatively because you've already invested in visits and treatments there, despite the evidence of good care in the future.

I could go on and on. At the moment of writing this book, science is aware of approximately 185 biases that influence the human mind.

These biases work beneath the surface of consciousness and affect almost every aspect of our lives, from the mundane to the critical, without most of us even realizing it. But understanding these biases is key to navigating the complex landscape of human thought and perception, allowing us to make more informed and deliberate choices.

And while unconscious biases can have a harmful effect—manifesting in serious issues like workplace harassment and obstructing diversity efforts—they also can play a positive role in the brief window in which perceptions are formed and professional imprints are made. In this narrow but critical space, you can harness the power of these biases to your advantage.

By being aware of them and intentionally presenting yourself in a manner that aligns positively from the vital first moments, you can influence others to see you in a more favorable light. This doesn't mean manipulating perceptions dishonestly but rather ensuring that the genuine and best aspects of your professional identity are what shine through and resonate most.

For the practice we just visited if, upon your arrival, the receptionist had briefly looked up and acknowledged you with a smile, making it clear they were wrapping up important work for another patient's care, your impression might have been different.

Maybe the receptionist could have offered you a glass of water or a cup of coffee while you had to wait. The unkempt nails may have faded into the background, overshadowed by a meticulous uniform and the courtesy of an instant greeting. You might have thought, "This practice is really dedicated to each patient's privacy and care." As you took your seat, the receptionist's professionalism might have cast a positive light on the surroundings, making the waiting room's imperfections seem less significant; instead, you might have noticed the beautiful paintings by a local artist on the wall. When the doctor arrived promptly, the efficient manner could have been seen as a sign of a well-run practice that values your time, turning a potentially negative first impression into a positive reflection of the practice's standards.

Now, let's translate these insights into the world of sales leadership. As a sales professional, you are constantly engaging with prospects or clients, team members, colleagues, and stakeholders who are forming impressions of you from the crucial first interaction. Just as a patient's perception of a medical practice can be swayed by subtle cues and unconscious biases, your professional imprint is being shaped by a myriad of factors, many of which you may not even be aware of.

Consider potential clients walking into your office for a meeting. From the moment the clients step through the door, their minds are processing information and forming judgments. Are the sales materials and product samples well-organized and easily accessible? Does your office reflect a modern, professional environment with up-to-date branding and visuals? Are you demonstrating a keen understanding of their specific industry needs from the start? Do you seem prepared, and were you on time for the meeting?

Each of these elements contributes to the clients' overall impression of you and your organization. If the sales materials are outdated or the product samples look worn, the clients' confirmation bias may kick in, reinforcing any preexisting doubts about your product's quality or your attention to detail. On the other hand, if the materials are fresh, current, and professionally presented, this positive anchor can set the stage for a more favorable interaction.

As the meeting progresses, the clients will continue to assess you based on a range of factors, from your appearance and body language to your communication style and expertise. Any perceived flaw, such as a lack of familiarity with their recent market trends, inconsistent follow-up on prior communications, or even a slight hesitation when answering a technical question, can trigger the horn effect, causing the clients to view your overall performance negatively.

Anchoring bias will ensure they cannot let go of that initial impression, and selection bias will compel the clients to focus on every little flaw.

They might notice if you frequently check your watch or phone during the meeting, if your demo device runs into technical issues, or if there are typos in your printed materials. If not managed properly, these small details, while seemingly insignificant, can overshadow the positive aspects of your pitch.

Self-serving bias might come into play when the clients think, "We always end up meeting sales professionals who oversell and underdeliver," making them feel even more justified in their negative assessment, even if you are doing your best.

The illusion of control will make the clients feel like they could have avoided this unsatisfactory experience if only they had chosen to meet with a different sales professional or organization. They think they had control over the situation, and that misplaced belief adds to their frustration.

In each of these instances, the clients' unconscious biases are shaping their perception of you and your organization. By being aware of these biases, you can take proactive steps to ensure that every aspect of the clients' experience is positive and professional, from the initial greeting to the final handshake.

To combat these unconscious biases and ensure that your professional imprint is a positive one, it's essential to be intentional about every aspect of your presentation. This means paying attention to the details.

But it's not just about avoiding negative impressions, it's about actively creating positive ones. By going above and beyond in your interactions with prospects or clients—anticipating their needs, providing exceptional value, and delivering on your promises—you can harness the power of unconscious biases in your favor. This means you are using the clients' unconscious biases to your advantage, which means you are not just imprinting a good impression, you are crafting an exceptional one.

To stand out in a sea of sameness is to go above and beyond the norm, to offer the unexpected in ways that positively disrupt and dismantle preconceived notions. It's about embodying excellence in every action and interaction and turning the ordinary into the extraordinary. The issue, then, isn't simply about being noticed; it's about being unforgettable. How can you truly stand out? The answer lies not just in what we do but in how we do it—with intention, with difference, with a touch of the remarkable.

For example, if you take the time to thoroughly research a client's business before a meeting and come prepared with tailored solutions, you demonstrate a level of dedication and expertise that can override any initial biases. If you follow up promptly after the meeting with additional resources and a personalized thank-you note, you reinforce the positive impression and make yourself more memorable. In addition to having your sales materials set out perfectly, you could mark the pages that are relevant to the clients' specific needs and highlight key sections that address their pain points.

Instead of a generic presentation, you could create a customized slide deck that includes industry-specific data, case studies relevant to their business or industry, and even a few slides that reference recent news or developments within their organization. You could incorporate elements that resonate with your clients' business. For instance, if you are meeting with a tech company, you could wear a sleek, modern smartwatch that subtly showcases your alignment with their industry's cutting-edge nature. Alternatively, if you are meeting with an environmentally focused company you might wear clothes made from sustainable materials. After the meeting you could send a personalized thank-you along with a small thoughtful gift related to the discussion—perhaps a book on a topic they mentioned.

The key to crafting a strong professional identity is to be aware of the unconscious biases that may be influencing your prospects' or clients' perceptions and to actively shape those perceptions in a positive direction.

By consistently presenting yourself with professionalism, expertise, and a commitment to excellence, you can stand out in a crowded field and build lasting relationships based on trust and credibility.

Remember: every interaction is an opportunity to reinforce your professional imprint and to leave a lasting impact on those around you. By being mindful of the power of unconscious biases and using that power strategically, you can elevate your sales leadership and achieve greater success in all your professional endeavors.

Stand Out for the Right Reasons

In the competitive landscape of modern workplaces where stakes are high and distinction is paramount, standing out is more than a personal goal, it's a professional necessity. Excellence is the new norm across industries. Sales leaders aiming to succeed must transcend the ordinary.

The truth is, "good" doesn't cut it anymore. Good is the baseline, the expectation. To be perceived as a leader—and to make a significant impact—you can't afford to simply fit the mold. Average blends in, and by blending in, you become invisible.

Think of the game Tetris. For some readers, Tetris is a nostalgic nod, a digital relic from the days of clunky, handheld gaming devices. But for those of a younger generation, it's a classic that's being rediscovered on smartphones and modern gaming platforms. No matter the version you're familiar with, the objective is the same: to rotate and align falling blocks to complete lines.

But what happens when the line is completed? It disappears. This is a triumph in Tetris, but in your career, it's a warning. When you align too perfectly with current patterns, you risk becoming part of the background—another completed line that serves its purpose and then vanishes into the sea of sameness.

When sales leaders stand out, they do so by transcending the ordinary. They become the piece in Tetris that not only fits but also starts a reaction, changing the landscape, challenging the status quo, and igniting new possibilities.

Standing out means being the architect of your perception, crafting your professional identity with intention, and making choices that set you apart in the professional sphere. It's about proactive distinction—carving out a space where your individuality and unique approach to your career resonate unmistakably. This requires being the memorable piece that doesn't just fill a gap but creates a new path for others to follow.

You might be thinking, "Well, is it always good to stand out?" For a pop star, standing out from the crowd in any way always brings positive returns. Whatever gets their name mentioned in the press will help sell their records. For any entertainer, standing out from the crowd, regardless of the reason, is also good to an extent. If they get on the evening news simply because everybody thinks they have done something out of order, they've won the game.

But in the professional universe, standing out for its own sake is a terrible idea. In the professional space, there's a great way to stand out, and there's a bad way to stand out.

The surest path to standing out in the best way is to consistently do these three things:

- **First, be your very best self.** Bring your unique strengths and personality to the forefront.

- **Second, embody and uphold the highest values of your organization.** Serve as a living testament to its mission and principles.

- **And third, don't just meet expectations, surpass them.** Strive to go above and beyond what's anticipated, delivering a performance that's not just good but exceptional.

The bad way to stand out is . . . well, any other way.

It's this commitment to excellence that will distinguish you in any profession.

Imagine if you walked into a doctor's practice and were greeted not just by a friendly receptionist but by a wave of innovation. The receptionist, with a welcoming nod, directs you to an interactive kiosk. It's an engaging check-in experience where you can personalize your visit, choosing room ambience settings from temperature to lighting to the background music. In the waiting area you're immersed in an environment designed for comfort and education. You instantly notice a refreshment bar, a gesture of hospitality that goes beyond the expected. Here, the receptionist offers a selection of herbal teas and nutritious snacks, transforming the waiting time into a moment of relaxation and nourishment for body and mind.

In your hands, a tablet becomes a window to wider knowledge. With an augmented reality application you explore health topics in a way that's interactive, immersive, and personalized to your health journey. Posters on the wall spring to life, providing a depth of understanding that pamphlets could never match. Amidst this, a subtle scent fills the air. The receptionist explains it's aromatherapy, intentionally chosen to create a calm atmosphere. It's a thoughtful touch that eases the inherent tension of waiting for a medical appointment. Instead of outdated magazines, the area features an exhibition of local artists' works. With art therapy books to peruse, the space is transformed into a sanctuary that indulges your senses and promotes healing.

At every turn, this practice has gone above and beyond. Even feedback is revolutionized. With a real-time device, you can express your level of satisfaction, empowering you as a partner in the healthcare experience. Later in the day, the doctor even personally calls to check on your progress instead of delegating the task to administrative staff. It's a continuous loop of communication, ensuring that you feel valued as an individual.

This practice has redefined what it means to stand out, ensuring that from the moment you walk in to the last farewell, your experience is anything but average.

As a sales leader interacting with your sales team, you also must reimagine what "exceptional" looks like and redefine what it means to be a remarkable sales leader. In your client interactions, you should be equally bold in separating yourself from the pack. Don't just sell products, sell extraordinary experiences that create memorable emotional connections. In your interactions with your team, this means leading by example and fostering an environment where excellence is the standard. This involves more than just guiding your team members in sales techniques; it's about inspiring them to embody the same level of dedication and personalization in their interactions.

But standing out isn't just about grand gestures, it's also about the small, consistent actions that build trust and credibility over time. It's about being responsive to client inquiries, even outside of business hours. It's about remembering personal details and using them to create a more personalized interaction. It's about following through on your promises and delivering results that exceed expectations. In a world where prospects and clients are bombarded with countless options and competing offers, it's these personal touches that can make all the difference. By creating an experience that is tailored and memorable, you give your prospects and clients a reason to choose you over the competition and to keep choosing you, time and time again.

So, as a sales leader, your challenge is to find ways to infuse every interaction with a touch of the extraordinary. Whether it's through innovative technology, personalized attention, or a commitment to going above and beyond, your goal should be to create a professional imprint that is unmistakably yours.

Remember: standing out isn't about being the loudest voice in the room; it's about being the most valuable. It's about bringing your unique strengths and perspectives to the table while also embodying the best of what your organization has to offer.

By consistently striving for excellence—in your appearance, your interactions, and your results—you create a powerful professional imprint that sets you apart. You become the sales leader that prospects or clients seek out, the one they trust to guide them to success.

So embrace the opportunity to stand out. Be bold in your vision, meticulous in your execution, and unwavering in your commitment to excellence. In doing so, you not only elevate your own career, but you also set a new standard for what it means to be a leader in the world of sales.

When Details Speak Loudest

In a world brimming with competence (and competition), where good has become the standard, the nuances of excellence whisper the secrets of distinction. Sales leaders who stand out are often those who understand that mastery lies in the eloquence of details. It's the fine print and the subtleties that can amplify a voice in a symphony of sameness.

The same principle applies to the professional imprint you leave. In your look of leadership, it's the attention to detail that speaks volumes. It's the crisp dress shirt or the perfectly tailored suit that projects authority, or the elegantly simple briefcase that showcases your sophistication. It's the polished shoes, subtly gleaming from beneath a conference table, that hint at a refined and thoughtful choice. It's the well-kept notebook with its neatly aligned edges, whispering of your methodical approach to your work. It's the gentle click of a quality pen, the unspoken ally of your thoughts during meetings. It could be the unique business card that reflects a personal identity or the thoughtful office decor that signals innovation. On a company website, a photograph that captures you engaged in a dynamic client discussion or mentoring your team sends a powerful message of collaboration. A professional headshot on your LinkedIn profile speaks volumes about how seriously you take your role.

These nuances collectively weave the narrative of a sales leader's commitment to their field and their inherent role as a trailblazer. These are the silent yet potent languages of excellence, the dialects of distinction that resonate with others.

In my keynotes I often illustrate how details can significantly influence judgments by sharing a fascinating video based on an actual study. The research involves twins who are dressed identically for various professional settings, such as two police officers, two managers, or two doctors. They sit side by side, looking completely alike in every way, but with one crucial difference: one of them is chewing gum.

As the study unfolds, participants are seated in front of the twins and asked a series of questions: "Which of them would be more likely to give you a parking ticket?" or "Which of them would be more inclined to give you a raise, or fire you if you asked for one?" The questions delve deeper into the twins' perceived social lives with participants speculating about which twin gets invited to more parties or has more friends, both real and imaginary. Even their supposed sex lives come under scrutiny.

Perhaps surprisingly, most individuals favor the gum-chewing twin across every scenario. The presence of that seemingly insignificant detail—a chewing gum—is enough to sway perceptions and create an entirely different narrative around each twin.

Of course, in reality, the relationship between a minor detail and these various outcomes is not so simple or clear-cut. Nevertheless, the study, which was later used in an advertisement video for a chewing gum brand, provides a compelling illustration of how easily our perceptions can be influenced by minor, often irrelevant factors.

As sales leaders, it serves as a powerful reminder of the need to be mindful and in control of the subtle details that can shape others' perceptions of us, sometimes in ways we might not anticipate or intend. It underscores the importance of being intentional about every aspect of our professional identity, from our appearance and conduct to the way we communicate and interact.

In the same vein, it's the finer details of presentation that can cause sales professionals to stand out—and be remembered—for less favorable reasons, be it the overly casual hairstyle that might be perceived as too laid-back for a client meeting; a palette of colors more befitting of a fashion runway than a corporate setting; the jewelry that clinks and clatters distractingly during presentations; a bold fashion statement that might overshadow the substance of a pitch; a shirt buttoned improperly that can seem careless; a tie that's a bit too loud; an overpowering cologne; or a laptop covered in an array of personal stickers that could undermine the organized professional identity we aim to project in a client meeting. All these details, however small, could overshadow expertise and intent and inadvertently shift the focus away from a sales leader's professional contributions.

It's these memorable yet incongruent details that could lead someone like Jennifer to recall an individual, not for their sales acumen but for their sartorial choices and think, "Ah, yes, that's the person with the strikingly vivid tie."

Is this fair? No. But humans, including you and me, are built to think this way.

Let's go back to another experience in a medical practice. Decades ago I found myself in need of a physical therapist to treat my back pain. The internet was a distant dream then, and I recall the quaint process of selecting a practitioner based solely on insurance coverage and the luck of the draw in a paper telephone directory. Yes, I know this dates me. Some readers might not even remember a time before Google, but there was one.

At my appointment I stumbled into a place that felt more like someone's home than a clinic. I navigated through a cluttered living room adorned with an eclectic assortment of plants, art, and odd collections—a creative chaos. Finally, I arrived at the treatment room, painted in sterile mint green and housing one of those physical therapy treatment tables enveloped in disposable paper.

Right there on that paper, which I thought was there for hygienic reasons, my eyes caught an unexpected sight—the remnants of a chicken bone. You read that right: the remains of what once was a chicken wing. Despite my initial shock—and I wish I could say I left instantly—I found myself discreetly disposing of the evidence in the therapist's trash can.

Moments later the therapist entered with a friendly greeting and an apology for his absence due to a quick lunch break between patients.

I don't remember much about the treatment itself. To be fair, it might have been wonderful. His medical analysis might have been on point, and his treatment plan might have made sense. But did I ever return? No.

Or take the case of my former dentist, who undoubtedly excelled in his dental work. But every time I reclined in his treatment chair, my attention was drawn to his complexion. It was clear he struggled with severe acne, a medical condition influenced by a variety of factors, as you know. Yet despite this understanding, I couldn't help but wonder why my dentist hadn't sought out treatments to alleviate his condition, especially as a medical expert himself.

Every visit to his office left me grappling with conflicting thoughts. On the one hand I admired his expertise in dentistry. On the other, I couldn't shake the feeling of discomfort caused by the visible signs of his untreated acne.

Or consider my first-ever therapist, whom I sought out during the pandemic. Our initial consultations, spanning the first half of the year, unfolded virtually with screens serving as our meeting ground. Our conversations provided much-needed support during those trying times. When the opportunity arose to finally meet in person as the world slowly reopened, we both were eager to see each other face-to-face.

It was during that first in-person meeting that I couldn't help but notice she was a flagrant nail-biter. Although she didn't engage in the habit in my presence, the telltale signs were evident.

It may seem like a minor detail, one easily overlooked amidst the patience, calmness, and guidance she had provided me, but from that moment on I found myself unable to shake the thought: how could someone visibly grappling with such stress and discomfort evident in the damage inflicted upon her nails effectively assist me in overcoming the mental challenges I faced? As time passed, I found myself hesitating to return, ultimately choosing not to do so without articulating the reason to her.

Have you ever walked into a boardroom only to be subtly irritated by the sight of someone's overly casual attire that left you questioning their performance? Or perhaps you've sat in a client's office and noticed the leftover coffee cups, each stained mug a silent testament to countless meetings and deadlines or, perhaps, a sign of a chaotic rhythm of work that made you wonder about their capacity to handle one more task or deadline.

Can you recall a time at a fancy restaurant when the waiter's stained shirt painted a picture at odds with the establishment's refined aura? Think back to the trainer at a sales seminar whose brilliant insights were momentarily overshadowed by the typos in their slide deck. Or the real estate agent who showcased pristine homes while their car, cluttered with personal belongings, narrated a separate story of chaos. Or the financial advisor whose expertise seemed inconsistent with their outdated, unprofessional website design.

As a sales leader, think of hosting a team training event in an unkempt, disorganized room, instantly undermining the professional identity you aim to command. Or walking into a big client pitch meeting disheveled after a long day on the road, compromising your team's credibility before you speak a word. A simple oversight, like using the wrong logo version in board presentations, can undermine you and cast unwanted scrutiny instead of inspiring stakeholder alignment.

The bottom line is that one incongruent visual detail can distract from the core value you offer, even if just for a split second.

But in the world of sales, one second of doubt is an eternity that competitors will seize.

These seemingly insignificant visual cues can speak volumes, often louder than words. Each wrinkle, stain, or out-of-place element becomes a character in the story we tell ourselves about the individuals we encounter, sometimes becoming a defining chapter that overshadows their skills and reputation and then transcends to the products or services they're trying to sell.

Successful sales leaders understand and accept that everything is rooted in the details. Those details can make us stand out for reasons both right and wrong. The challenge is that those details will be of different importance from person to person and occasion to occasion.

In your sales role, it's crucial to understand the "frame of attention"—the specific visual cues that draw particular focus, depending on your profession and the individuals you interact with.

For instance, hygiene is an extraordinarily important factor in the healthcare industry. A healthcare sales professional must not only dress professionally but also exude cleanliness and meticulous attention to personal grooming as prospects or clients will subconsciously associate their appearance with the standard of care they represent. Conversely, if you are selling technology, the emphasis might shift to how modern and innovative your appearance and materials are.

Understanding these frames of attention helps you tailor your appearance to resonate with what is most important to your prospects or clients, ensuring that every visual detail aligns with the message you aim to deliver. It allows you to control the frame of attention to your best advantage, even though you'll never be able to fully adjust to the expectations of the person in front of you.

Take, once again, the instances of the chicken bone, the acne, and the nail biting, which may not raise an eyebrow for some patients, but for me they were enough to influence my perception and my decision-making.

Yet, in contrast, I find myself in the care of a different therapist now. Despite her office being a vibrant collection of eclectic items and her appearance diverging from any conventional expectations, she has a remarkable ability to instantly create an atmosphere of safety, warmth, and comfort. With her, none of those details seem to hold any weight.

While it's impossible to cater to every individual expectation, demonstrating a consistent commitment to excellence will always work in your favor. Recognizing that each industry and client may prioritize different aspects allows you to strategically emphasize those details most likely to resonate.

Whether it's the precision of your attire, the quality of your materials, or the subtle personal touches that show your attention to detail, mastering those elements ensures that you present yourself as a competent and professional partner. After all, one jarring detail can be enough to consign you to the category of loser or create an unwanted distraction.

Yet despite the challenge of meticulously considering each of these minor aspects, doing so presents a remarkable opportunity for you. In the sales world where many professionals are deemed average, these subtle nuances allow you to stand out, and for all the right reasons. It's not about being perfect; it's about being intentional and consistent in your pursuit of excellence.

In the world of sales, where many professionals blend into the background, these details become your secret weapons. They are the brushstrokes that paint a picture of a leader who is meticulous, thoughtful, and committed to their craft.

Embrace the power of nuance and use it to your advantage. Be the sales leader who understands that, sometimes, it's the smallest things that make the biggest impact. Whether it's the way you carry yourself in a meeting, the precision of your follow-up emails, or the thoughtfulness of your client gifts, let every detail reflect your dedication to excellence. In doing so you'll not only stand out, you'll also set a new standard for your team and for what it means to be a leader in the world of sales.

The ABCDEs of Your Professional Identity

As we piece together the many small interactions we have, a clear picture begins to form. This picture is your professional identity. Think of it as a puzzle in which each piece, no matter how small, has its own place and reason for being. Each detail works together to show who you are as a sales leader, and no element exists in isolation; rather, the elements interlock to form the complete picture that others perceive.

Your professional identity encompasses a multifaceted blend of choices you make—small and large—that shape how you're perceived and valued in your role. And this professional identity is the sum of your choices in the following five areas:

- Appearance
- Behavior
- Communication
- Digital footprint
- Environment

Here's an easy way to remember these five key elements: just think "ABCDE."

APPEARANCE: Your appearance is your first opportunity to make a statement without saying a word. It's the canvas upon which your personality is painted. From the moment someone lays eyes on you, they're subconsciously processing a wealth of information about who you are and what you represent.

Let's start with your body image, the first thing others notice about you. Whether you're tall or short, slim or sturdy, these physical attributes shape the initial perception others form. But it's not just about the shape or size of your body; your overall health, both physical and mental, also radiates through your appearance. A vibrant glow of vitality or a worn-down facade can speak volumes about your well-being.

Clothing is your armor in the battlefield of first impressions. The fit, brand, style, quality, patterns, and colors of your clothes silently communicate your taste, personality, and attention to detail.

Accessories are the finishing touches that add flair to your ensemble. Whether it's a statement watch, a sleek tie, or a pair of polished shoes, these embellishments speak volumes about your personality and style.

Maintaining your wardrobe is an often overlooked aspect of personal presentation. Well-kept garments demonstrate your commitment to professionalism and, again, attention to detail.

Your personal grooming is the final touch that completes your appearance. Skin care, hair care, dental hygiene, and nail maintenance all contribute to your overall presentation.

Your appearance is a silent language that sets the stage for meaningful connections and interactions.

BEHAVIOR: At the core of your behavior lies your attitude—the vibrant colors that illuminate your outlook on life, ranging from sunny optimism to cloudy pessimism. Your attitude not only sets the tone for your interactions but also serves as a compass to guide you through the twists and turns of both your career and your life.

Adding depth to your behavior is your charisma (or lack thereof), that magnetic personality that draws others into your orbit.

Navigating this rich tapestry of behavior requires emotional intelligence, the wisdom to read between the lines and steer gracefully through the intricate labyrinth of human interaction.

But no masterpiece is complete without a sturdy foundation of ethics and morals, the bedrock upon which your character stands. And as you navigate the vast canvas of human interaction, diplomacy and courtesy should be your guiding stars.

With your behavior, you not only enhance your effectiveness as a sales leader but also weave a landscape of lasting relationships and meaningful connections.

COMMUNICATION: At the heart of communication lies active listening, the art of tuning in to others. Through active listening you not only hear the words spoken but also understand the emotions and intentions behind them.

Adding depth to your communication are your body language and facial expressions, the nonverbal and silent-yet-eloquent language of gestures, postures, and movements. Your body and face speak volumes, conveying emotions and attitudes that words alone cannot express.

And what melody is complete without your voice—the instrument you play every single day? Your voice features a range of tones, pitches, and cadences, from the gentle lilt of persuasion to the commanding resonance of authority, and each vocal element adds depth and richness to your message.

Words are the essence of communication, and your language palette is the tool you use to craft your message.

Yet it's not only what you say but how you say it that shapes the narrative of your communication. Your communication habits, whether empathetic and concise or passive and manipulative, set the tone for your interactions, guiding the flow of every conversation and shaping the dynamics of relationships. Your accent or dialect may add richness and diversity to those conversations. Finally, your written communication is the ink that flows through the veins of our interconnected world.

By intentionally weaving together these elements of communication, you create a masterpiece of connection.

DIGITAL FOOTPRINT: Your digital footprint is like a breadcrumb trail scattered across the internet; each crumb leaves its mark on your online reputation. From intentional actions to those unwittingly left behind, each interaction shapes not only your digital presence but your offline persona.

At the heart of this trail lies email communication, a digital handshake that speaks volumes about your professionalism and reliability.

Similarly, your mobile communication offers glimpses into your accessibility and efficiency.

Venturing into the topic of social media with your posts, comments, likes, and shares can enhance your online reputation, positioning you as a credible and insightful voice within your digital community.

In virtual meetings your digital footprint takes on a new dimension, showcasing your adaptability and professionalism in remote settings.

Meanwhile, chats and forums serve as arenas for digital discourse where your contributions reflect your expertise, engagement, credibility, and influence within online communities.

The frequency, savviness, and authenticity of your digital interactions shape your unintentional footprint, influencing how you're perceived in the digital realm.

By actively managing and curating your digital presence, you can craft a compelling message that aligns with your professional aspirations and values, leaving a lasting impression on those who encounter your digital trail.

ENVIRONMENT: Your environment isn't just where you are, it's the vibrant backdrop against which your professional journey unfolds. It's filled with both tangible and intangible elements that shape your daily experiences and leave an indelible mark.

Your network, for example, isn't just a list of contacts; it's a living ecosystem that provides support, fosters collaboration, and unlocks doors of opportunity at every turn.

Then there are the spaces you inhabit, the places where you live and work. They're more than just physical locations; they're sanctuaries of productivity, creativity, and inspiration.

And let's not forget the journey itself, the daily commute, the occasional getaway, and the leisure pursuits that recharge your batteries.

From the thrill of exploration to the tranquility of downtime, these experiences add color to the canvas of your professional life, infusing it with excitement, balance, and rejuvenation.

Your environment isn't just a backdrop; it's a character in the story of your professional journey, shaping the plot and influencing the outcome at every twist and turn.

So take a moment to look around. What do you see? How does it make you feel? And most important, how can you optimize it to support your goals, reflect your values, and lead you toward success and fulfillment?

In the end, your professional imprint is a mosaic of countless pieces, each one carefully chosen and placed to create a masterpiece that is uniquely you. From your appearance to your behavior, your communication to your digital footprint, and your environment to your overall presence, every element plays a vital role in shaping how you're perceived and valued as a sales leader.

And while our focus quickly shifts to an individual's visual appearance, it is essential to recognize that these visual cues extend far beyond the person. The meticulous design of a slide deck, the organized and inviting layout of an office space, the neatness of a desk, and the condition of a company vehicle all send visual cues and, hence, contribute to your overall appearance. Each of these elements reflects a commitment to detail and excellence.

And while an impeccable look—both personal and extended—can open doors, it is your behavior and communication that will sustain those connections. Simply looking great is insufficient; proving your worth with your actions and words must consistently support the professional identity created by your appearance.

Furthermore, in today's digital age, your digital footprint holds immense relevance, as it often determines the capability to engage in meaningful in-person interactions. Your digital presence frequently serves as the first impression prospects or clients and partners encounter, one that can determine if you will ever meet them in person.

And last, your environment is often the most underestimated factor. While it is widely acknowledged that surrounding yourself with the right individuals is crucial, in practice, many of us continue to associate with individuals who neither enhance our professional identity nor contribute positively.

Your professional identity is a holistic representation that is shaped by various interconnected elements. Only by being intentional about each piece of the puzzle can you craft a professional identity that is authentic, compelling, and unforgettable. So take the time to carefully consider each element of your ABCDE. Choose pieces that reflect your values, your strengths, and your aspirations. And then, with every interaction and every decision, let your professional imprint shine through.

Remember: your professional identity is your most valuable asset. It's the key to opening doors, building relationships, and achieving your goals. So nurture it, refine it, and let it be a source of pride and inspiration, not just for you, but for all those whose lives you touch.

Internal and External Consistency

Consistency is the backbone of any credible professional identity. The key is to ensure your appearance, behavior, communication, digital footprint, and environment all sing the same tune. You can't present yourself as reliable and trustworthy in your clothing but behave unpredictably or unprofessionally during interactions. You can't curate a digital presence that conflicts with who you are in the real world.

Surrounding yourself with luxury and glamour while aspiring to a reputation of humility and service sends mixed messages. Exhibiting professional conduct during business hours but behaving recklessly or inappropriately outside of work leads to confusion. Using a professional tone in verbal communication but producing written communications full of errors or lacking clarity undermines your perceived competence.

Only when all elements of your professional identity align does the message of who you are and what you stand for become unmistakable, compelling, and memorable. This consistency also extends beyond your personal presentation, both within your organization and in the wider world.

Your internal professional identity pertains to how you present yourself, behave, and communicate within the intricate ecosystem of your organization. This identity encompasses interactions within your sales team and department, collaborative projects with cross-functional teams, and consultations with colleagues or top management. Sales leaders who demonstrate unwavering consistency in their professional identity within their internal sphere earn the respect and trust of others within their organization. Think about the ripple effect of your actions, how your commitment to excellence can inspire your team, enhance collaboration, and drive overall organizational success. Reflect on how every decision, every interaction, and every presentation contributes to the larger narrative of your leadership.

Your external professional identity, in contrast, pertains to how you represent yourself and your organization to external stakeholders. Each public interaction, whether it's a client presentation, a networking event, or a speaking engagement at an industry conference, is a stage upon which your professional identity is showcased. The perceptions you create in such moments extend beyond your personal reputation; they influence how your organization and its leadership are viewed in the broader market. Those external interactions are not just about selling a product or service; they are about building trust, establishing authority, and reinforcing your organization's brand and values. Imagine the power you have as you craft your organization's reputation, because each of your interactions is a testament to your dedication to professionalism and your strategic acumen in navigating the complexities of the business world.

Consistency in your appearance, behavior, communication, digital presence, and environment, both internally and externally, reinforces trust and credibility, enhancing both your personal reputation and that of the organization. But as a sales leader this principle, while seemingly straightforward, encompasses a complex and nuanced challenge that extends beyond individual effort.

Achieving personal consistency is the foundation, but the true test of a sales leader's capability lies in ensuring that this consistency permeates the entire team. The challenge is not only to maintain your own standards but to inspire and embody those standards for all team members. When the entire sales team adheres to agreed-upon norms, it fosters unity and professionalism, creating a cohesive and credible front that significantly enhances the organization's image. Conversely, any deviation by team members can lead to confusion, undermining team cohesion, the organization's reputation and, ultimately, your professional identity as a leader.

It's essential for members of your sales team to understand that their appearance, behavior, communication, digital presence, and environment inside and outside of their respective organizations reflect on the organizations they represent. And although many team members may diligently adhere to internal protocols and standards within the workplace, there can be a tendency for some to inadvertently overlook these standards outside of professional settings.

At any given time your sales team may encounter prospects or clients, stakeholders, or community members outside the professional setting. It's crucial team members maintain the highest level of excellence in those interactions—anytime, anywhere, and with anyone—to uphold their organization's reputation.

If this resonates with you as a familiar challenge, another chapter of this book will delve into strategies and techniques for effectively addressing these challenges with your team, providing tips to support you in conducting these sensitive conversations.

For now, picture this: you're presenting at a major industry conference. You've spent months preparing, honing your pitch, and perfecting your presentation. You step onto the stage, and all eyes are on you. In that moment your appearance, your behavior, your communication—everything about you—is a reflection of your organization.

Now imagine there's a member of your sales team in the audience. They're not presenting, but they're still representing your organization. And let's say, hypothetically, that this team member has chosen to attend the conference in clothing that's more suited for a casual night out than a professional event. Or maybe they're engaged in behavior that's less than professional. In this scenario, the inconsistency between your professional presentation and your team member's actions creates a discordance that can undermine your credibility as a leader and the reputation of your organization.

Or picture this: one of your team members brings everything you could wish for to in-person meetings with prospects and clients. Every day they show up as the picture-perfect professional, displaying impeccable behavior and communication. Yet, one day you encounter your team member's social media posts and find them filled with unprofessional or controversial content. This inconsistency can severely impact your reputation as a leader as well as the organization's reputation, as it suggests a lack of oversight or a disconnection between professional and personal standards.

Only when everyone is on the same page and presenting a united front of excellence, it strengthens the overall impact of your organization. But when there are inconsistencies, it creates cracks in the foundation of your professional identity. It sends mixed messages about what you and your organization stand for, and that can lead to confusion and mistrust among prospects, clients, and stakeholders.

So how do you foster consistency within your sales team? It starts with clear communication and expectations.

Your team members should understand the importance of maintaining a consistent professional identity, both within the organization and in external settings. This understanding can be achieved by having clear guidelines for their appearance, behavior, communication, digital footprint and, to the extent you can, even their environment. And it means leading by example, consistently demonstrating the professional standards you expect from your team. It means fostering an environment where team members feel valued, supported, and motivated to do their best work. It means providing opportunities for growth and development and recognizing and rewarding outstanding performance.

When your sales team feels fully invested in the success of the organization, they're more likely to take pride in their work and to consistently present themselves in a manner that reflects positively on the organization.

Consistency in your professional identity is about more than just looking the part. It's about embodying the values and standards of your organization in every interaction, every communication, and every decision. It's about creating a seamless alignment between who you are, what you stand for, and how you present yourself to the world. And when you achieve this consistency, both personally and across your sales team, you create a powerful professional identity that inspires trust, credibility, and respect. You position yourself, your sales team, and your organization as leaders in your field, setting the standard for excellence and professionalism.

So as you navigate the complex world of sales leadership, strive to align every element of your professional identity and work to foster this same consistency within your team. In doing so, you'll create a professional identity that is unforgettable, unshakeable, and reflective of the leader you are and the organization you represent.

Chapter 3
Leaders Look Confident

Confidence Isn't Thinking You Are Better. It's Realizing You Have No Reason to Compare Yourself.

Chapter 3:
Leaders Look Confident

What is confidence? What does it mean to look confident? And why do these factors matter for a leader? Those are complex questions, but they have answers.

Confidence, in the broadest sense, is not merely about possessing a firm belief in your abilities or the decisions you make. It transcends the boundaries of self-assurance to encompass an aura of competence, empathy, and unwavering authority that inspires trust, respect, and a sense of security among all stakeholders—colleagues, team members, prospects, clients, and the wider community. In the professional world where decisions often carry the weight of life-altering consequences, the confidence of a leader becomes a cornerstone.

In the high-stakes arena of sales, few qualities are more essential than an unwavering sense of confidence. This inner belief in your ability to adapt, persist, and succeed is a prerequisite for thriving amidst the constant rejections and uncertainties inherent in the profession.

Researchers often have explored this vital link between confidence and sales performance. Studies by Robert S. Heiser at the University of Maine and David McArthur at Utah Valley University affirm that confidence and enthusiasm are prerequisites for exceptional selling. Their findings suggest the most successful sales professionals exude an air of confidence that allows them to remain adaptive and resilient in their approaches.

Similarly, a research paper by Guangping Wang at Louisiana State University indicates sales professionals with higher levels of confidence tend to outperform their less confident counterparts. An inner reserve of belief empowers the self-confident to invest greater effort, even when facing repeated setbacks and naysayers.

Confidence, the cornerstone of successful sales leadership, often finds itself besieged by a multitude of enemies. Those adversaries, lurking in the shadows of the high-stakes world of sales, can chip away at even the most self-assured leader's confidence. Let's explore some of those confidence saboteurs and how they uniquely impact sales leaders.

Comparison—The Thief of Joy and Confidence: In the hyper-competitive world of sales, leaders often find themselves in a relentless cycle of comparison, measuring their performance, achievements, and even their perceived value against those of their colleagues. Such comparisons can be insidious, subtly eroding confidence and fostering feelings of inadequacy. Despite achieving remarkable results, if you constantly scrutinize your metrics against the top performer in your organization, follow the leaderboard, compare quarterly sales figures, and monitor every other benchmark against your own success, you will chip away at your own sense of accomplishment. It's natural to compare results, especially in the sales arena, yet understanding that comparison is a thief of confidence is crucial for sales leaders. True confidence stems not from outshining others but from recognizing and celebrating your own unique path, strengths, and accomplishments. It's about fostering an internal validation that is resilient to the external pressures of comparison.

Rejection—The Constant Companion of Sales: In sales, rejection is an ever-present specter. Few other professions demand that individuals face such a constant barrage of "noes" as an integral part of their daily lives. Each rejected pitch, each unanswered call, and each lost deal can feel like a personal failure that slowly erodes the confidence of even the most seasoned sales leader.

The cumulative weight of those rejections can be overwhelming and lead to self-doubt. But true confidence in sales leadership lies in reframing rejection as an opportunity for growth, learning, and resilience. It's about understanding that each "no" brings you closer to a "yes" and that the ability to persevere in the face of rejection is the hallmark of a confident and successful sales leader.

Imposter Syndrome—The Inner Critic: Imposter syndrome, the nagging feeling of being a fraud despite evidence of success, is a common confidence killer among high-achieving sales leaders. The higher they climb, the more they may feel like they don't belong or that their accomplishments are the result of luck rather than skill. This inner critic can be especially loud in the sales world where success is often quantified and publicly celebrated. Sales leaders may find themselves questioning their own expertise, doubting their ability to replicate their successes, or fearing they'll be found out as inadequate. Overcoming imposter syndrome requires a conscious effort to internalize achievements, acknowledge the hard work and talent that led to success, and embrace the idea that you deserve your position and accolades.

The Rapid Pace of Change—Staying Ahead of the Curve: The world of sales is in constant flux with new technologies, changing customer preferences, and shifting market dynamics. For sales leaders, staying confident in the face of these rapid changes can be a daunting task that can erode confidence and lead to a sense of being perpetually behind the curve. Maintaining confidence in this environment requires a commitment to continuous learning and a willingness to experiment and adapt.

Quota and Pipeline Pressure—The Weight of Expectation: In sales, the pressure to meet and exceed quotas is relentless. The constant scrutiny of pipeline metrics, forecasts, and revenue targets can be a significant source of stress and self-doubt. The weight of expectation, both from upper management and from your team, can cause you to question your decisions and your ability to steer your team to success.

When quotas are missed or pipelines look lean, it's easy for confidence to waver. But true confidence comes from focusing on the process rather than the outcome, trusting in your ability to adapt and lead through challenging times. It's about maintaining a steadfast belief in yourself and your team, even amidst the ups and downs of the sales cycle.

Confidence is a complex construct, built from a mosaic of internal and external factors. While some of these enemies of confidence are not unique to sales, they take on a particular intensity within the high-stakes, fast-paced world of sales leadership. Combating these deep-rooted adversaries requires a multifaceted approach, one that addresses both the internal and external aspects of confidence. While the psychological battle against these enemies is ongoing, there is one powerful weapon in a sales leader's arsenal that can help shield against these confidence saboteurs: your visual appearance.

At first glance, the link between your look of leadership and confidence may seem superficial, a mere matter of dressing the part. But the impact of your external presentation on internal confidence is far more profound. In the face of the myriad challenges and self-doubts that plague sales leaders, a powerful look of leadership can serve as a suit of armor, a tangible reminder of your professionalism, competence, and readiness to lead.

Think of it as a way of showing up for yourself even on the days when confidence is in short supply. By taking the time to curate a look of leadership that exudes capability, authority, and self-assurance, you're not just influencing how others perceive you, you're engaging in a powerful act of self-affirmation. You're sending a message to yourself that you are worthy of investment, that you are prepared to face the challenges of the day, and that you are capable of handling whatever comes.

Moreover, by focusing on the aspects of your appearance that are within your control, you're creating a bulwark against the confidence-eroding effects of comparison.

Rather than measuring yourself against others' visual standards or succumbing to the pressure to conform, you're defining your own professional identity. You're cultivating a look that authentically reflects your unique strengths, values, and leadership style.

Of course, this is not to suggest that a well-crafted appearance is a panacea for all the enemies of confidence. The psychological work of building and maintaining confidence is ongoing and multifaceted. But by leveraging the power of your look of leadership as part of a holistic, confidence-boosting strategy, you're giving yourself an advantage in the daily battle against self-doubt.

So as we explore the "look of leadership" in the pages to come, let's approach visual appearance not as a superficial consideration but as a potent tool in the confidence-building arsenal. In a world where confidence is continually under siege, your appearance can be a powerful ally, a tangible expression of your inner strength and resilience.

Let's first explore the internal dimension of dressing with confidence. It's a universally acknowledged truth that when we look good, we feel good. This isn't shallow vanity but a reflection of how closely intertwined our self-esteem and self-perception are with our external appearance.

Clothes do more than just cover us up; they can make us feel good or uneasy, especially at work. Researcher Kim K. P. Johnson and her team, responsible for the article "Dress, Body and Self: Research on the Social Psychology of Dress," found that when professionals dressed right for their job, they felt more certain of themselves. They associated psychological discomfort with wearing inappropriate dress for work.

Mary Katherine Brock's research also confirms that young sales professionals' confidence is heavily influenced by the clothes they wear. Even color seems to matter, as Craig Roberts and his research team point out, because certain colors, such as red, can boost confidence.

You might remember the research I mentioned earlier by Hajo Adam and Adam D. Galinsky who introduced the concept of enclothed cognition, which means what we wear can change the way we think and feel. Let's take a closer look at how they performed this study. Their research focused on the significance of wearing white coats in the medical arena. Their study delves into how this attire impacts mental processes. They discovered that wearing a white coat can sharpen a person's focus. But the effect varied based on the described purpose of the coat: white coats labeled as belonging to doctors enhanced focus more than those described as painters' coats. This finding indicates that the influence of clothing on cognitive function hinges on both the symbolic association and the physical act of wearing the garment.

In sales leadership, the armor of a well-considered wardrobe serves not only as a physical outfit but as a psychological booster. What we decide to put on every day can shape how we feel about ourselves and how we interact. It's not just about looking good; it's about feeling good too.

Just think of it for a moment: how often have you felt a dip in confidence because of a poorly chosen outfit? Have you ever instantly cringed when a prospect mentioned they found your social media profile, knowing it includes an outdated picture? Have you ever walked into an important client meeting only to realize your shirt has an obvious stain? Have you ever found your confidence wavering due to unkempt hair or a rushed shave? Have you ever noticed how a cluttered background visible on a video call detracted from the professional identity you aimed to project? These visual missteps, small as they may seem, can significantly influence your confidence and, consequently, how you are perceived.

On the flip side, the external dimension of dressing with confidence concerns how you are perceived by team members, colleagues, prospects, clients, and the broader community.

Sales professionals exuding confidence through their visual look subconsciously garner more attention.

Their confidence captivates, signaling expertise worth listening to. Or for those working in your organization, a sales leader's confident presence isn't just appealing, it sets an aspirational bar. When leaders take pride in their appearance, it reinforces an empowering culture of achievement.

Even the broader professional community will make unconscious judgments about a sales organization's stature based on how confident its ambassadors appear. Thus, impressive visual confidence burnishes the reputation of the collective.

The inescapable reality is that projecting a confident presence significantly elevates how your leadership abilities are judged. It shapes impressions of credibility and competence from every angle. That's why mastering the art of looking confident is an essential tool for earning the trust required to exert effective influence as a sales leader.

And confidence is undeniably contagious, especially when it emanates from someone in a leadership position. As a sales leader, the confident aura you cultivate and the intentionality your refined presence radiates inspires your entire team's psyche and performance.

When you carry yourself with confidence, it instills in your sales professionals a sense of pride in who they represent. They begin emulating the high standards you embody, feeling motivated to show up as their best selves. Your confidence becomes their confidence.

Conversely, any glimpses of insecurity or half-hearted efforts toward your own professional identity can breed uncertainty in the ranks. If the leader seems uninspired, it gives permission for team members to underperform and make excuses.

The confidence you curate through every nuance of your professional identity—from your razor-sharp decision-making to your neat and trendsetting outfits—becomes the driving force propelling your entire sales team toward greatness. It's the underlying source code that transforms teammates into self-actualized brand ambassadors.

As the adage goes, "They will never care how much you know until they know how much you care." The contagious effect of a leader's confidence is, perhaps, the most pivotal force for elevating everyone's performance.

Leaders Are Confident about Their Body

Let's start our discussion about confidence by ignoring all the things you can buy at a department store or online and focus on the suit you were born with: your body.

Sales professionals who are comfortable in their own skin command a presence that is authoritative, reassuring, and confident. By embodying confidence in their physical selves, sales leaders can set a powerful example for colleagues, team members, and the community.

Recognizing the body as a fundamental aspect of your identity and a vessel through which you offer leadership is the first step toward deeper self-confidence. You need to acknowledge your unique body characteristics—your strengths and your limitations—and embrace them as parts of who you are.

Although there certainly are some tricks when it comes to dressing your body, you'll never be able to fully change the fundamentals: someone short will never be tall. Someone overweight will never appear skinny. This acceptance is not resignation but a celebration of diversity and your individuality, so your focus should be on your body's health.

Even so, research does provide insightful correlations between height, weight, and leadership perception. Sylvia Ann Hewlett and her team surveyed college-educated professionals and senior executives about executive presence.

They found that women are judged more critically by their weight whereas men are more likely to be judged by their height. Of those surveyed, 16 percent said it's important for men to be tall compared to just 6 percent for women.

Height is often perceived as a silent herald of leadership. It's associated with authority, confidence, and dominance. But the intrinsic value of leadership is not measured in inches. Even though height may be a factor, enduring leadership is built on the foundation of competence, empathy, and integrity. These are qualities that transcend physical dimensions.

And the reality is that height is a fixed attribute, although visual strategies such as posture, wardrobe choices, and the strategic use of footwear can subtly influence the perception of height. But remember, opting for shoes that hamper your natural walk can do more harm than good. It's about striking a balance—wear what elevates your confidence without compromising your comfort.

In contrast, weight, which might be perceived as a reflection of personal discipline and lifestyle, often becomes a topic of discussion in relation to credibility and authority. In various professional spheres, particularly those with a focus on health, fitness, or overall well-being, weight can carry connotations of personal discipline and lifestyle, influencing perceptions of credibility and authority.

For instance, consider industries such as personal training, healthcare, or nutrition where professionals often serve as role models for healthful living. In these fields the expectation might be that personal appearance aligns with professional advice. Similarly, sales leadership roles that demand a high degree of discipline and self-control might also scrutinize physical fitness as a proxy for those traits. In such industries the unspoken norms suggest that, in the minds of others, maintaining a certain physique may be intertwined with professional effectiveness.

This scrutiny around physical fitness as a proxy for diligence and self-mastery could extend to other sales leadership roles as well. For example, in the luxury goods, high-end hospitality, or elite concierge services sphere prospects or clients could perceive a sales leader's personal upkeep and athletic conditioning as emblematic of the attention to detail they'd expect when purchasing prestigious offerings and exceptional experiences.

The connotation is that if they can't maintain high standards for themselves, how can they deliver it for coveted clientele? Similarly, in high-finance industries like wealth management or institutional investment sales where building and maintaining client trust hinges on projecting impeccable judgment and personal accountability, a sales leader's fit and energetic presence may be viewed as an unspoken credential that signals integrity and commitment to best practices.

The bottom line is there are professional areas where influential leaders must personify the premium ideals, values, and lifestyle aspirations underlying the products or services they represent. In those markets, physical fitness can become subconsciously intertwined with credibility and authority in highly subjective yet impactful ways.

In public opinion, unlike height, weight is seen as a variable and is frequently more directly linked to perceptions of health. Here, sales leaders have a dual role: to model a commitment to well-being and to challenge the stereotypes that unjustly conflate physical appearance with professional competence.

Bias related to weight manifests in two opposing but equally damaging stereotypes: those who are heavier may be perceived as lacking self-control or health awareness, whereas those who are thinner may face misjudgments of being too delicate to manage the stress and responsibilities of sales leadership positions. Both stereotypes are unjust and overlook the individual's actual capabilities and contributions.

The research of Patricia V. Roehling and her team highlights how obesity affects perceptions of promotability, demonstrating that obese candidates are often seen as less suitable for promotions compared to individuals with other physical conditions.

This bias also extends to leadership perceptions where obese individuals are significantly underrepresented in top positions within Fortune 100 companies. Additionally, studies by T. L. Brink and supported by Eden B. King reveal that obesity can significantly influence views of a person's leadership abilities.

A study by Joseph A. Bellizzi and Ronald W. Hasty found that leaders broadly viewed obese professionals as less suited for challenging, client-facing territories that demand constant engagement and presence than their colleagues who were not obese. Interestingly, the discriminatory effects were lessened for roles involving minimal face-to-face customer interactions, such as inside telephone positions. Perhaps most disconcertingly, the research indicated that obese professionals faced harsher disciplinary actions from their leaders for ethical breaches or other misconduct than did colleagues who were not obese. It is as if the perceived lack of self-control over their physical appearance prejudiced decision-makers into assuming a lack of self-control over professional judgment and behaviors.

But despite the impact of weight on professional perceptions as highlighted by various studies, the most crucial factor is your own relationship with your body weight, because it significantly influences your confidence. This internal perception of self-worth and assurance can override external biases and shape how you're viewed in sales leadership and professional capacities. Hence, for those seeking to align their weight with their health goals and professional identity, options to do so are presented next.

Carry your weight with poise and confidence. Do so no matter the number on the scale. But keep in mind that the right fit of clothing can significantly affect how you and others perceive your weight. Ill-fitting clothes can seem to add pounds or create an unflattering silhouette that is distracting. Conversely, well-tailored clothes can enhance your look of leadership, contributing positively to your confidence and overall perception. The key is a strategic selection of clothing that fits impeccably, thus avoiding adding unnecessary bulk or implying a lack of attention to detail, both of which can detract from your professional identity. And ignore any outdated and oversimplified methods of categorizing body shapes.

You are more than an "apple" or a "pear"—you are a sales professional, a leader, a force, and an individual whose worth is defined by accomplishments and abilities, not by the contours of a silhouette. Your shape does not confine your potential; your presence, your expertise, and your actions carve out the real shape of your influence and impact. This advice, although once popular, not only pigeonholes you but also overlooks the nuances of personal style. It disregards the fact that whereas some individuals may wish to downplay their "pear" shape, others may want to accentuate it. No one-size-fits-all concept can dictate whether you should highlight or downplay your shape. Your body, your rules—your style should be a reflection of you, not a fruit comparison chart.

Opt to lose or gain weight. The focus should be on health rather than solely on aesthetics. Positive changes in weight can lead to a boost in self-esteem and an improvement in how you are perceived. And as you probably know, this process should be undertaken with mindfulness, ensuring the journey toward weight change is sustainable and reflects a genuine commitment to your well-being. When considering a weight change, it's essential to approach the subject holistically. It's not just about the number on the scale but about nurturing a lifestyle that promotes overall well-being. Weight management can be empowering and affirming, especially when accomplished through methods that prioritize nourishment, energy levels, and inner balance. It's about finding what feels good and sustainable for your body and lifestyle. A well-nourished body supports a sharp mind, essential for decision-making and endurance through long days. Moreover, exercise and a balanced diet are known to improve mood and reduce stress, contributing positively to your professional identity.

Finally, it's about inclusivity in health and wellness, recognizing that healthy bodies come in all sizes and that the objective isn't a specific aesthetic but a state of health in which you feel most vibrant and capable.

This approach helps ensure the journey toward any weight change is sustainable while reinforcing the idea that leadership is embodied in a myriad of forms.

In the end, the measure of a sales leader is not taken from physical attributes such as weight or height but from the impact you make, the individuals you mentor, the teams you empower, and the contributions you make to your field and your organization. Observable physical characteristics are superficial metrics that do not reflect the depth and breadth of your influence and capabilities. The essence of your sales leadership radiates from a core of integrity, expanse of expertise, and elevation of your goals and vision. But if your outward appearance can amplify your inherent confidence, it's a resource worth harnessing. Embracing your weight or changing it proactively does not undermine your authenticity; rather, it underscores your self-awareness and the deliberate cultivation of your professional identity. It's not about misrepresentation but about presenting yourself in a manner that reflects your best qualities and intentions. After all, sales leadership is a performance art, and every leader is both the sculptor and the sculpture of their professional identity.

Leaders Are Confident about Their Age

Another influential factor in shaping perceptions is age, which is often correlated with experience and wisdom on one end and energy and innovation on the other. It bears a psychological weight, influencing both the self-perception of sales professionals and the expectations of those they work with and serve.

The spectrum of age in the professional sales world is broad and diverse. On one end are the seasoned sales leaders whose years are viewed as a compendium of expertise, a living library of knowledge and experience garnered through years of dedication and hands-on work. Their age is often associated with a profound understanding and a reassuring presence that commands respect in any professional challenge.

On the flip side, youth in the professional sales arena are lauded for their connection with agility, both mentally and physically. Younger sales professionals are often seen as the vanguard of innovation, bringing fresh perspectives from recent education and a zeal for progressive methodologies. Their age represents a drive for momentum and an ambition to innovate and expand the horizons of their respective fields.

Yet these perceived roles are not without their complications. Seasoned leaders may feel compelled to demonstrate ongoing relevance in rapidly changing industries, whereas emerging leaders often work to assert their authority and gain trust within hierarchies that have historically valued longevity.

Each stage of a sales leader's journey is accompanied by its own set of perceptions and expectations, both self-imposed and from external sources. It's within this intricate landscape that leaders must establish their age-appropriate professional identity, capitalizing on the strengths that come with their experience while challenging any perceived age-associated constraints.

Age, much like height and unlike weight, is an immutable number, a marker of time that, contrary to popular belief, has no direct correlation with success. Across the spectrum of history, leaders have emerged at various stages of their lives, showcasing that age is not a determinant of capability. Success in sales leadership is age agnostic; instead, it is reliant on the unique value and experience each individual brings to their role.

The key to navigating age is embracing it, owning your years with confidence. This means focusing on the richness of your experience, the depth of your knowledge, and the unique value you add to your team and your organization; it means celebrating milestones and using your accumulated wisdom to influence and inspire.

For younger professionals, this means the focus should be on leveraging the fresh perspectives, energy, and adaptability that come with youth.

It's about demonstrating a willingness to learn and innovate. It involves using your unique insights and enthusiasm to drive change and inspire, proving that age is just a number and that potential and capability are not confined by years.

Nevertheless, it's human nature to wish to be perceived, at times, as younger or older than you are, but a challenge arises when efforts to alter your age's perception lead to inauthenticity. Yes, visual elements can be used to suggest a more youthful or mature image, but they should be approached with moderation.

Excessive attempts, such as dressing overly younger or older than your years, extreme dieting or fitness regimens that are unsustainable, the use of heavy makeup to conceal natural features, the adoption of fashion trends that do not align with your personal style or age, or overindulgence in plastic surgery can convey a lack of confidence in your natural progression through life, a message particularly conflicting in sales leadership where authenticity and trust are paramount. These efforts, despite aiming to enhance your appearance may, instead, project a sense of insecurity, and they often backfire.

When sales leaders resort to extreme measures to alter their age appearance, it can overshadow their actual competencies and achievements. It's a delicate balance between using visual elements to slightly improve your confidence and adjust your age's perception and overstepping into the territory where those elements detract from your authenticity.

View your age as an asset, not a barrier, and aim to present yourself in a way that highlights the intrinsic value you bring to your role. Resist succumbing to societal pressures about age. In embracing your years with dignity and self-respect, you also set a positive example for your colleagues, team members, and prospects or clients that it's not the number of years in your life or career that define your value but the quality and impact of your performance.

Leaders Are Confident about Their Gender Identity

It will come as no surprise to you that gender dynamics play a significant role in leadership perception. Wait a minute . . . Please pause right here.

If you're thinking of skipping this chapter, please reconsider. Navigating gender dynamics is a critical skill for every leader, regardless of gender.

Traditionally, nurturing roles were often seen as women's domains whereas positions demanding authority were typically reserved for men. In the modern professional landscape, these outdated stereotypes are being actively contested and redefined. But despite significant progress, subtler shades of these stereotypes linger, manifesting in nuanced biases and expectations that persist beneath the surface of our evolving workplace culture. It's an ongoing process to root out these remnants and move toward an equitable professional environment.

In research conducted by Janice Fanning Madden at the University of Pennsylvania, an insightful spotlight was shone on the sales teams within large brokerage firms. In those environments where income is intrinsically tied to performance and commission, an imbalance was uncovered. Women, despite demonstrating equal aptitude in achieving results, were frequently handed accounts with less potential than those of their male counterparts.

Likewise, research from Joanna Barsh and Lareina Yee by McKinsey and Company confirmed that invisible barriers are holding women back rather than overt sexism alone. The "Howard vs. Heidi" case study, spearheaded by Frank Flynn, an associate professor at Columbia Business School, delves into the intricate dance between competence and likeability that women leaders often must navigate. Participants in the study assessed the profile of a candidate—described identically in all respects but name—first as Howard, then as Heidi. Howard emerged from this scrutiny not only as competent and effective but as someone subjects found likeable and who they were eager to collaborate with.

Conversely, Heidi, despite being recognized for her competence and effectiveness, was not met with the same warmth or enthusiasm for future partnership. This singular shift in gender naming laid bare an underlying bias: high-achieving women are often subjected to a stricter social ledger than men are, one where their success could diminish their likeability, a dilemma less frequently faced by their male counterparts.

In examining the impact of gender on perceived leadership effectiveness, research by Charles M. Futrell in the *Journal of Personal Selling and Sales Management* revealed some sobering realities. Futrell's study asked sales professionals from an industrial manufacturer to evaluate different leadership styles portrayed by sales managers on video.

The key finding was that the sales professionals' assessments were influenced heavily by the portrayed manager's gender, regardless of the specific leadership approach displayed. Unconscious gender biases colored evaluations; the same behaviors were viewed as more or less effective based solely on whether the manager was a woman or a man.

Significant barriers to gender equity have been dismantled over the years, often under public scrutiny. That success has led to tangible consequences for organizations, but it's the subtler, less visible forms of inequality that persistently erode the foundations of equity. These forms can be harder to detect and even more challenging to address because they often go unnoticed in the public eye despite being deeply embedded in workplace cultures and attitudes. Hence, women in sales still must consistently navigate these gender-based perceptions in an effort to ensure that the quality of their work and their professionalism are the primary criteria for evaluation, not their gender.

As a woman in sales leadership, you also may encounter the double-bind paradox in which you're expected to be nurturing yet decisive, authoritative yet compassionate. The key to overcoming this issue is to embrace your gender identity with confidence and showcase your unique leadership style.

This approach means not feeling pressured to conform to traditionally masculine modes of leadership. By cultivating a personal leadership style that encompasses both empathy and assertiveness, you can redefine what it means to lead with influence and integrity, regardless of gender.

Although gender bias is often discussed with a focus on women, it's crucial to recognize that men are also subjected to rigid societal expectations. When we discuss gender bias, we usually talk about women; when we think of race, we usually think of people of color. Other groups go unexamined and unanalyzed. Defined by a narrow interpretation of masculinity, for example, men are sometimes pressured to be decisive, tough, and unyielding, leaving little space for vulnerability or emotional openness. These standards, instilled from a young age through family, education, and media, can be restrictive and damaging.

In the sales environment, these pressures manifest in various ways. For instance, male sales professionals might feel compelled to adopt an overly aggressive sales approach, believing that showing any sign of hesitation or uncertainty could be perceived as weakness. Males may avoid asking for help or feedback, fearing it might undermine their image of competence and control. During negotiations, the expectation to be tough and unyielding can lead to missed opportunities for collaboration and compromise. The pressure to constantly project confidence can prevent male sales leaders from expressing doubts or discussing challenges openly with their teams, which can stifle growth and innovation.

It's vital to consider the full spectrum of gender dynamics, understanding that true equality challenges constraints for all genders. This includes nonbinary and transgender sales leaders who often must navigate a world that is still learning to understand gender beyond the binary. Their visibility in sales leadership roles is, itself, an act of courage and representation. For nonbinary and transgender sales leaders, the challenge is often about being seen and respected for their professional capabilities without their gender identity overshadowing their skills and contributions.

In the sales arena, for instance, during client meetings or presentations nonbinary or transgender sales leaders might encounter inappropriate questions or comments about their gender identity, diverting attention from their professional message. There can be instances where their authority is questioned or undermined due to a lack of understanding. Additionally, nonbinary and transgender sales professionals may face difficulties in networking events where traditional gender norms dominate, making it challenging to build relationships on an equal footing.

By focusing on professional acumen and advocating for an environment in which all are evaluated on their abilities and contributions, we can help ensure sales leadership is an area defined by the quality of work, not by the gender identity of those providing it. Each of us has a role in spearheading the shift toward policies and norms that honor gender diversity and that embodies empathetic and inclusive leadership. Alongside such efforts, it's vital to cultivate an awareness of how gender bias still quietly casts its net through often unspoken microaggressions, shaping our interactions and workplace culture in subtle yet profound ways.

Embracing your own gender identity as part of your sales leadership is a profound statement of acceptance that sets a powerful example. The key lies in being comfortable in your own skin and using your unique experiences to inform and enhance your leadership approach beyond your gender. At the core of your professional reputation should always be an unwavering commitment to excellence and the quality of leadership you express. In such an environment, gender can become one of many aspects of a sales leader's identity, not a hurdle to overcome but a facet that contributes to a leader's distinct perspective.

For your look of leadership, this means nurturing a self-image that resonates with your values and convictions. It's about harmonizing your external presence with your inner identity, ensuring that your professional identity reflects your competence. Let your gender identity enhance, not define, your sales leadership style.

Leaders Are Confident about Their Style

Style is not simply about the clothes you wear or the fashion trends you follow; it's a broader expression of your identity. A leader's visual style is a representation of who they are, offering a glimpse into their personality without uttering a single word.

Style isn't about chasing the whims of fashion, nor is it defined by the price tag or the prestige of luxury brands. It's not about molding yourself to fit the silhouette of the moment or echoing the masses. Style doesn't insist on perfection; it's not a static, one-size-fits-all formula. It's not about dressing to impress or a costume you put on for approval. True style transcends seasonal trends and societal expectations; it's an individual expression that doesn't wane with time or shift with tides of public opinion.

Although it's essential to respect the professional environment and those within it, there's room to weave in distinctive elements that set you apart. The primary concern is striking a balance: your style should never overshadow your competencies but complement and enhance your professional narrative.

Your style could reflect the distinctive elegance of a custom-tailored blazer, the strategic selection of an accessory, or the timeless charm of a statement piece. It's in the carefully chosen tie clip that commemorates a personal triumph, the glimpse of an unexpected pattern on a shirt, or the addition of a brightly colored pocket square that brings life to a traditional outfit. It's the distinctive design of a watch or the deliberate choice of vibrant socks that signals a meticulous eye for detail. These elements should not scream for attention but should invite intrigue and respect.

Style is not just about preference in color or fit; it's also about the message you want to send. And that message is rooted in the values you want to project—confidence, approachability, innovation, tradition, creativity, or care—and how they are encapsulated in your appearance.

Sales leaders who have defined a unique style exude a distinctive presence that transcends mere clothing.

Their strong sense of style reflects their personality and authority while acting as a visual signature that makes them easily recognizable and memorable. But sales leaders who master their style also understand that going overboard can be counterproductive. It's not about pushing boundaries to the extreme but about pushing them just enough to be intriguing and, above all, being true to yourself. Your style should not distract; it should fascinate. It should not raise questions; it should assert confidence.

Defining your personal style is a journey that many find challenging. Unlike pursuing a specific role or niche in your career, which may be influenced by passion, skill, or opportunity, style is more abstract and deeply personal, lacking a definitive guide.

The question, "What's your style?" can often leave sales professionals pondering in silence. In fact, style is such a complex concept that it requires many questions to be answered before you can confidently define it, questions including these:

- Does your style amplify your voice?
- How does your style make you feel about yourself?
- How does it affect your confidence?
- Are there elements that make your style memorable?
- Does your style incorporate elements of your personality?
- Can your style further evolve while maintaining your core identity?
- Does it reflect your leadership capabilities?
- How does your style influence your team's perception of you?
- Is your style practical and functional for your activities?
- How does your style align with your organization's values and culture?
- How does your style adapt to different contexts?
- How does your style bridge or speak to diverse client backgrounds?
- How do your style choices reflect your commitment to quality and attention to detail?

Your style composes a story of who you are and what you stand for without uttering a single word. Only by answering the underlying questions can you begin to craft a style narrative that is not only unique but that aligns with your authentic self, which can lead to curating a style and professional brand that consistently and coherently communicate who you are at your core.

There is no shortcut to developing a sense of style.

In their haste to avoid the introspective and challenging journey of defining and maintaining their unique style, many resort to clichéd solutions that, ultimately, undermine their efforts. Take, for instance, the common practice in the speaking world of dressing in your brand's colors, limiting yourself to wearing red simply because the logo is red.

This is not an expression of style; it is a superficial gimmick. Effective personal style transcends such facile shortcuts and demands a deeper, more thoughtful approach.

Consider sales leaders in the luxury automotive industry. Rather than relying on overtly car-themed accessories, they might incorporate more understated nods to their passion through high-end materials and refined aesthetics. Perhaps a silk tie with an elegant pattern reminiscent of the sleek lines and curves found in sports car design. Or a leather briefcase showcasing the same exceptional craftsmanship and attention to detail that goes into the brand's interior cabins. Even a timepiece selection that evokes the marriage of precision engineering and luxury finishes could underscore an appreciation for the product's essence.

Or imagine sales leaders in the fashion industry. They might use their style to showcase their creativity and eye for detail, perhaps through the use of bold color combinations or unexpected textures in their clothing choices. Such elements not only set those leaders apart, the elements also demonstrate their expertise and connection to the world of fashion.

Even in more conservative industries, such as finance or law, sales leaders can express their personal style in subtle ways.

A well-tailored suit in a unique color or with a distinctive lining, a pair of statement shoes, or a carefully chosen piece of jewelry can convey a sense of individuality and confidence without detracting from the professional identity.

The key is finding ways to authentically express industry zeal and personalized flair through sophisticated choices that enhance rather than distract. It's about cultivating a coherent, intentional style alignment between individual and organizational image without compromising taste or propriety.

By avoiding heavy-handed literal themes, sales leaders demonstrate a more nuanced understanding of how to embody a brand's identity with the polish and self-assuredness that allows their genuine passion and expertise to shine through in elegant yet impactful ways.

So take the time to explore and refine your personal style. And then wear that style with confidence and pride. Let it be a reflection of the sales leader you are and the impact you aim to make in your industry and beyond.

Chapter 4
Leaders Look Authentic

The Art of Standing Out
While Fitting In,
Without Disappearing.

Chapter 4: Leaders Look Authentic

In a world where perception often trumps reality, the pursuit of authenticity has become a rallying cry for leaders across all industries. Yet, what does it mean to be an authentic leader in the high-stakes landscape of sales? Is it about unfiltered self-expression, or is there a more nuanced approach that balances personal identity with professional expectations? Ignoring your environment and the context in which you operate can lead to a dangerous misconception about authenticity, one that is especially prevalent in the advice, "You do you!" This notion suggests that being authentic means you can do, say, or wear whatever you want, regardless of the situation. It's advice that, admittedly, I have both given and received. But this advice fails to recognize the importance of aligning your authentic self with the expectations and norms of your professional setting. When you disregard the context and operate solely on the principle of you do you, there is a risk of coming across as tone-deaf or even disrespectful. In the world of sales, where building trust and credibility is paramount, this can be a costly mistake. It can give the impression that you don't care about anyone or anything, anywhere, any time.

Let me share some uncomfortable truths with you.

Authenticity is not an excuse for disregarding norms. The reality is that authenticity does not exist in a vacuum. As a sales leader, you operate within a complex network of relationships, expectations, and social norms.

While it's important to stay true to your core values and beliefs, you also must recognize that our actions and self-expression have an impact on those around us.

When you use authenticity as a justification for ignoring professional norms and expectations, you risk damaging the very relationships and trust that are essential to our success as leaders. Prospects, clients, and stakeholders have certain expectations of how a sales leader should conduct themselves, and when you disregard those norms in the name of authenticity, you can come across as unprofessional, untrustworthy, or even arrogant.

This doesn't mean that we need to completely suppress our individuality or conform to a rigid set of rules. Rather, it means we must find a way to express our authentic selves within the framework of our professional context. It's about understanding the needs and expectations of those we work with and adapting our approach accordingly, but without compromising our core values.

There is no such thing as one singular authentic self. The notion that we each have one "authentic self" is a lie.

The reality is that we each play numerous roles. We're parents, siblings, children, friends, neighbors, colleagues, and sales leaders. Each of those roles demands a different facet of our personality and presentation. To be successful, you need to adapt your authentic self to the context of each role in terms of your appearance, behavior, and communication. Imagine interacting with your children the same way as with your prospects or clients, or speaking to your parents as you would to your life partner. Imagine wearing the same outfit in the gym and at work. Although there may be a consistent thread of core values and beliefs that defines you, the expression of your authenticity will vary depending on the situation.

Authenticity, then, is not about a rigid adherence to a single, unchanging self in all contexts. The focus is on being true to your core values while also possessing the flexibility to effectively navigate various environments.

In sales leadership, authenticity means finding harmony between your private persona and your professional identity, ensuring that each role you play is infused with your values. This harmony allows for different versions of authenticity that are considerate of both your own self-expression and the expectations of those around you. It's not about concealing who you are; it's about respectfully acknowledging the part you play in each role of your life and doing so with sincerity and professionalism.

Authenticity is not a fixed state. Many professionals believe that once they discover their authentic self they're set for life. They think that authenticity is a destination, a place they never have to leave. But the truth is, authenticity is a journey, not a final destination. As we navigate through our careers and our lives, we are constantly growing, learning, and evolving. Our experiences shape us and our relationships change us. Our perspectives shift. As a result, our understanding of ourselves and how we express our authenticity also evolves. What felt authentic to us in our twenties may not feel the same way in our forties or sixties.

That's why it's crucial to regularly reassess and adjust our authentic expression. We need to take the time to check in with ourselves, to ask if the way we're presenting ourselves to the world still aligns with our core values and beliefs. It's a process of continuous self-discovery and self-alignment, one that means recognizing that what made us authentic leaders in the past may not be what makes us authentic leaders in the present or future.

Authenticity is not an excuse for being unfiltered. There's a common misconception that to be authentic you must share every detail of your life and thoughts, holding nothing back. But this couldn't be further from the truth. Authenticity doesn't mean you have to reveal every aspect of your life to everyone. It's okay to have boundaries and to choose what you share and with whom. It's about being honest and genuine in your interactions, not about oversharing or being unnecessarily transparent.

Moreover, authenticity should be tempered with empathy and consideration for others. It's not about being blunt or hurtful under the guise of being "real." It's about expressing yourself in a way that is true to you but also respectful of those around you.

Authenticity, while essential, does not come without these boundaries, particularly in a professional context and particularly if you want to succeed. These boundaries are often crafted by the implicit expectations and unspoken scripts that permeate every industry and society at large. Like invisible guardrails, they guide and shape perceptions, influencing how others view and interpret your actions, words, and appearance.

In sales leadership these expectations can be particularly pronounced. Prospects or clients, colleagues, and stakeholders all have preconceived notions of what a sales leader should look like, sound like, and act like. These scripts, while rarely explicitly stated, carry significant weight in how your authenticity is perceived and received. And your appearance can either confirm or challenge these scripts. Aligning your appearance with these professional expectations isn't about diminishing your authenticity; it's about reflecting your authentic self within the framework of your role.

During my keynotes I present participants with various images of individuals dressed in professional attire. I then pose a question to the audience: "Which of these individuals would you entrust with your legal battles, your computer setup, or the education of your children?" The responses are predictably consistent, underscoring how quickly we form perceptions based on appearance. My audience's inner dialogue might go something like this: "The sharp lines of that charcoal-gray suit, the impeccable white shirt, and the red tie exude a strategic and commanding presence—that's got to be the lawyer." Next to that person is someone in smart casual attire—a coat, a light shirt without a tie, and slacks. "Clearly, that's the IT expert." Then there's someone in a light, pastel dress that flows softly, the kind that suggests kindness and a nurturing spirit; "surely, she's the teacher."

It was those small, deliberate choices that created the look of leadership, that spoke before a word was uttered, that painted a picture of those individuals in their professional worlds while expressing their authentic selves in their roles. So let's examine how you, too, can strategically align your look of leadership with your authentic self.

Keywords Are the Keys to Authenticity

We all carry mental templates of various professionals, and while those templates might differ in detail, they share certain core attributes. The attire of the lawyer my audiences envision isn't chosen for its creative flair; rather, it's selected for the messages it conveys: reliability, authority, trustworthiness, and consistency. In the legal profession the keyword that resonates is "trust" not "creativity." Contrast the lawyer with the attire of a head of marketing in a multimedia firm or the head of a buying department in a retail company. While marketing and buying professionals also may wear a suit, the fabric may be more distinctive than that of a lawyer, featuring an eclectic pattern and unique style elements. Paired with a vibrant shirt and, perhaps, a brightly colored bow tie or standout accessories, their look would capture the essence of creativity, the keyword for marketing and buying.

Unveiling your industry-specific keywords and expectations. In every industry there exists some form of a mental "uniform"—a sartorial standard that may not be as overt and codified as those of police officers, firefighters, military personnel, or chefs, but it's implicitly understood. Those are the "perceived uniforms," an unspoken dress code shaped by societal expectations and assumptions about certain professions. Those perceived uniforms serve as a visual shorthand, helping forge an immediate connection between professional identity and public perception and allowing sales professionals to visually express their expertise and role within the industry.

You might ask, "So what are the expected keywords in my industry?" The answer lies in the collective expectations of all stakeholders—prospects or clients, partners, colleagues—who interact with sales leaders across fields. These keywords become the essence of the perceived uniform for each industry. They reflect the attributes that associates, colleagues, and prospects or clients alike associate with professionalism and expertise.

In B2B sales, the keyword "excellence" may be instantly expected and can be visualized, for example, through structured suits and conservative colors.

In creative industries, the keyword "innovation" might feature bold statements and eclectic pairings that showcase creativity in your appearance.

For those in sales for sustainable products, "eco-friendly" is key, and clothing choices made from earth-conscious materials can communicate a genuine commitment to sustainability.

In the dynamic world of sports sales, "energetic" and "team-oriented" pieces reflect a blend of strategy and action, mirroring the vibrancy of the industry.

Attire in the tech sales industry aligns with "cutting-edge" and "high-tech" themes, often incorporating sleek and modern elements that speak to the forward-thinking nature of the field.

Each of those keywords encapsulates an industry's or role's values and the expectations of those who interact with it. By carefully crafting a professional identity that aligns with those keywords, you can craft a professional identity that not only meets professional standards but that resonates with the unique characteristics of your field, thereby reinforcing your role and strengthening your personal identity. But defining keywords can be intricate because doing so is influenced by numerous factors that include your specific industry, the culture of your organization, your geographical location, and the diverse backgrounds of the clientele and colleagues you engage with regularly.

Defining your distinctive edge and personal keyword. The most authentic sales leaders understand that their professional identity is a powerful form of nonverbal communication. Through their chosen style they convey a narrative about who they are, and they're clear about the keywords that describe this narrative. Each keyword tells a part of their story, and each look confirms its essence. If your professional ethos is grounded in dependability, expertise, and commitment, your professional identity should reinforce those qualities. Alternatively, if you pride yourself on being bold, your choices might be more daring and innovative, reflecting a trailblazing spirit.

Have you considered the unique traits that define you in your sales role and how they translate into the visual messages you wish to instantly imprint? Reflecting on these defining traits that make you unique in your professional life and how these translate visually is crucial. Doing so allows you to pinpoint a style that not only makes you self-confident but also conveys the key messages you intend to communicate. It's a process critical in shaping not just any personal style but one that resonates with confidence and the professional identity you want to project.

Harmonizing your industry's expectations and your personal essence. Once your industry's (or organization's or profession's or specific role's) keyword and your personal keywords are established, the next phase is alignment, checking whether those keywords resonate with the ethos of your profession. If you are fortunate, the keywords you selected to describe your authentic self will align with the persona expected in your professional sphere. When there's a match, it can feel like a natural extension of your identity. Conversely, if there's a disconnect, it can manifest as a nagging sense of being out of place, prompting you to question why you feel like you don't quite belong.

These are the leaders who often find themselves at a crossroads, grappling with the tension between their authentic selves and the expectations of their roles.

They may feel like they're constantly putting on a mask, suppressing parts of themselves to fit into a mold that doesn't fit. This internal dissonance can lead to feelings of frustration, burnout, and even a loss of purpose.

On the flip side, when there's alignment between personal and professional keywords, those leaders tend to thrive. They exude a sense of ease and confidence in their roles, as if they were born to do what they do. Their authenticity shines through effortlessly, and they have a way of inspiring and motivating others simply by being themselves.

This alignment allows them to bring their whole selves to their work, tapping into a deep well of intrinsic motivation and passion. They don't feel the need to compartmentalize or hide parts of themselves because their authentic identity is not just accepted but celebrated in their professional context.

But achieving this alignment is not always a straightforward journey. It often requires a deep level of self-awareness, a willingness to reflect on your values and priorities, and the courage to make changes if necessary. It may involve seeking out roles, companies, or industries that better align with your authentic self, or it may involve working to shift the culture and expectations within your current environment.

Emerging from the myriad of possible keywords and attributes are seven distinct perception personas, each of which symbolizes a specific set of values and traits that sales professionals either naturally embody or are expected to adopt. These personas go beyond mere clothing choices; they represent the holistic professional identity that sales leaders are anticipated to uphold in their work and interactions. The seven personas can be categorized into two distinct types: your primary persona, which forms the core of your identity, and your secondary persona, which complements and enhances the primary one.

Your primary persona is akin to your DNA—it's the bedrock of your identity. It's reflected in the consistent strands of your character, coloring your instinctive choices and the way you inherently engage with the world.

Your secondary persona is more fluid, sculpted by the ebb and flow of your external experiences, age, education, preferences, and the continuous curve of personal and professional development. It grants you the flexibility to adapt, to mold your choices to fit the myriad of scenarios you encounter throughout your career and life.

Whereas your primary persona remains unaltered, steadfast in its authenticity, your secondary persona acts as a versatile complement. It doesn't overshadow your core; rather, it expands upon it, allowing you a greater spectrum of expression. Together, they form a cohesive identity that is both true to your essence and attuned to the nuances of your professional environment.

Before we embark on outlining the personas, it's important to recognize that these personas are not rigid classifications. They do more than just categorize us. They influence our perspective on the world and, consequently, these personas are often reflected in our external presentation—the clothes we choose, the hairstyles we adopt, and the accessories we carry, all of which are outward expressions of our inner narrative. It's also possible that you find yourself in more than one primary or secondary persona. (We'll examine this complexity later.)

It's also crucial to note that while I use elements of each persona's visual appearance to describe them, their traits also permeate into behavior, communication, digital presence, and environment. These personas are holistic, encompassing not just how we look but how we act, interact, and present ourselves in all aspects of our professional lives.

But it's often through our visual appearance that we realize the first strong indication of how these personas express their unique keywords. Their looks serve as the initial canvas upon which they paint the picture of who they are and what they stand for. Their visual appearance is like the book cover in the narrative of their professional identity, setting the tone and creating expectations for the interactions to come.

But just like in a book, their story goes beyond the cover. Their appearance is just the beginning. It's through their actions, words, and the way they engage with the world around them that the full depth and complexity of their persona is revealed. The personas are multidimensional, reflecting the authentic self that they bring to all aspects of their leadership role. For now, let's get started with the three primary personas.

The Explorer: Approachable and Relaxed

Explorers embody a spirit that is both adventurous and pragmatic, often reflected in a style that prioritizes comfort and practicality. They choose their wardrobe less for the latest fashion trends and more for functionality and durability.

Their attire is as ready for an impromptu client visit as it is for a casual business meeting: comfortable slacks paired with a resilient button-down shirt and sturdy footwear that speaks to a life in motion.

In their wardrobe you'll find clothes, many in earthy tones, that serve a purpose: utility jackets with pockets aplenty, fabrics that can withstand the elements, and colors that blend with the natural world. Maintenance is easy with a preference for clothing that endures the wear and tear of their sales adventures without demanding meticulous care.

Their approach to body image is straightforward and unpretentious. Their physique, whether it's conditioned by active pursuits or carries the robustness of a life well lived, is a testament to their experiences rather than a curated image.

In their world, the body is less a canvas for fashion and more a vessel for adventure, a mindset that brings a unique confidence and an unbothered attitude toward societal beauty standards.

When it comes to grooming, the Explorer favors a minimalistic approach. A touch of moisturizer for a healthy glow, a swipe of clear lip balm, and a simple hairstyle are all they need to maintain their natural look, ready for whatever the sales day may bring.

Their accessories, like the sporty watch on their wrist to the durable briefcase slung over their shoulder, are chosen for resilience and utility, echoing the Explorer's readiness for life's spontaneous sales adventures.

For hair and nails, Explorers opt for easy maintenance, prioritizing health and manageability. A simple, practical haircut suits their active lifestyle. Their manicure and pedicure are neat yet unfussy, often favoring clear polish or natural tones that don't show wear easily.

- **Keyword:** comfort
- **Perceived traits:** active, adventurous, casual, approachable, optimistic, energetic, natural, direct, spontaneous, enthusiastic
- **Perceived challenges:** disorganized, dull, graceless, mannerless, ordinary, unambitious, unpolished, weak

The Explorer persona can be particularly well-suited for sales roles that demand an approachable, down-to-earth presence and the ability to seamlessly transition between formal and casual client environments.

For example, in industries like consumer goods, sporting equipment, or outdoor recreation sales, the Explorer's adventurous spirit and utility-focused wardrobe choices can align perfectly with their target client base.

Similarly, when selling to small businesses, startups, or entrepreneurs, the Explorer persona's casual confidence and unfussy personal identity can foster an instant rapport.

Their lack of pretense signals accessibility—a trustworthy advisor in tandem with a client's hustle. It's a natural fit for those gritty, roll-up-your-sleeves sales environments.

Explorers also may thrive in sales roles within traditional manufacturing, industrial, or agriculture spheres. Their practicality legitimizes their hands-on capability in the eyes of prospects or clients. The sartorial resilience mirrors the durability and utility those industries value in partners and suppliers.

But true Explorers might struggle in highly formal and image-conscious industries such as high-end luxury goods, corporate finance, or executive-level consultancy, as these industries often require a professional identity. The Explorer's preference for comfort over high fashion may be seen as too casual or unrefined.

The Traditionalist: Trustworthy and Reliable

Traditionalists carry an air of timeless elegance, exuding a commitment to enduring styles that is immediately apparent. They aren't swayed by passing trends but are firmly rooted in classic fashion principles.

Envision them in attire that pays homage to the past—a well-tailored suit that defies the ebb and flow of fads, a crisp dress shirt that whispers decades of sophistication, or leather shoes polished to perfection.

In their wardrobe you will discover a carefully selected ensemble that defies the transient whims of fashion, featuring enduring quality and craftsmanship. Each item is tended to meticulously, ensuring their presentation is flawless while honoring their conservative sensibilities.

Their perspective on body image is in harmony with this classic sense of style. Traditionalists convey diligent self-care and a refined composure, regardless of body type. Their physique reflects a persona that upholds their values—subtle yet unmistakably dignified.

When it comes to grooming, Traditionalists opt for the timeless—a neat hairstyle, a clean shave or well-trimmed facial hair, and a subtle fragrance that serve more as a tribute to poise than a pursuit of the spotlight.

Their accessories are chosen with discretion, from the understated elegance of their cufflinks to the classic lines of their wristwatch. As for hair and nail care, they select styles that stand the test of time—perhaps a sleek side part or a classic manicure. Their nails are impeccably groomed, often in clear or neutral polish, complementing their wardrobe's timeless grace.

- **Keyword:** values
- **Perceived traits:** trustworthy, loyal, organized, practical, consistent, dependable, responsible, reliable, conscientious, appropriate
- **Perceived challenges:** authoritarian, boring, conformist, inflexible, elitist, predictable, reserved, uncreative

The Traditionalist persona resonates powerfully in sales roles that prioritize engendering deep client trust and unshakable credibility. Their commitment to timeless styling tends to be an asset when operating in more conservative, legacy-minded industries.

For example, in financial services sales like banking, wealth management, or institutional investing the Traditionalist's classic appearance helps foster perceptions of fiscal responsibility that are crucial for earning buy-in.

As account executives selling into long-established professional services organizations like law, accounting, or consulting partnerships, the Traditionalist persona aligns with conducting business with utmost formality and adherence to decorum.

Traditionalists also can thrive in certain B2B sales environments in manufacturing, energy, logistics, and other industries with long-entrenched and risk-averse corporate cultures. Their steadfast propriety helps engender immediate trust and credibility when navigating those companies' entrenched bureaucracies.

Any sales roles requiring an ability to impress budget authorities who deeply value custom, propriety, and hard-earned reputations over flashiness, the Traditionalist's persona conveys the ideal mix of experience and professional standards.

But Traditionalists might find it challenging to thrive in more fast-paced industries that value a cutting-edge approach. Traditionalists' adherence to classic and conservative fashion might be perceived as outdated or too rigid.

The Cosmopolitan: Sophisticated and Eloquent

Cosmopolitans are an embodiment of luxury and refinement, a sartorial symphony in which each element harmonizes with their sophisticated lifestyle.

Their wardrobe is a subtle murmur of opulence. Designer brands and lavish pieces are selected not merely for their aesthetic allure but also for their ability to broadcast an air of exclusivity and global sophistication.

Their wardrobe maintenance mirrors their dedication to a life well-curated with each garment receiving the meticulous care needed to maintain its premium appearance.

Their view on body image is anchored in elegance. Cosmopolitans consider their physique as a canvas for high fashion with each silhouette and contour gracefully adorned in fine materials. The manner in which they carry themselves—a synthesis of poise and self-assurance—enhances their impeccable taste in clothing.

When it comes to grooming, they strike the perfect balance between understated and impactful, crafting a visage that speaks of refinement and luxury. A perfect hairstyle, a hint of color in their accessories, subtle fragrance, and a well-manicured appearance adds just the right touch of sophistication.

Accessories for them are more than adornments; they are declarations of quality and craftsmanship that articulate their discerning preferences.

Their grooming, including hair and nails, follows the philosophy of "less is more"—as long as it's exquisite. Elegant hairstyles that frame their face and a manicure that boasts of subtle, neutral tones or a classic style. Those choices are intentional, serving not just as aspects of their personal upkeep but as integral parts of their social signature.

Every facet of their appearance, from meticulous skin care routines to the selection of a signature scent, is a conscious act in shaping an identity that vibrates with the core of high society.

- **Keyword:** quality
- **Perceived traits:** distinguished, proper, notable, cultivated, refined, meticulous, discerning, dignified, excellent
- **Perceived challenges:** arrogant, bossy, calculating, decadent, impersonal, intolerant, stiff, uncaring

The Cosmopolitan's refined, cultured persona lends itself exceptionally well to luxury and premium consumer product sales roles. Their sophisticated style and distinguished aura naturally align with the aspirational ethos of high-end retail, beauty, fashion, and other upscale experiential offerings.

Similarly, in industries like high-end travel or tourism, private aviation, or boutique hospitality sales, the Cosmopolitan persona's global sophistication and impeccable poise exude the jet-setting sensibilities and white-glove service standards those rarified experiences promise.

For real estate catering to affluent prospects, the Cosmopolitan's cultivated persona projects the precise elevated tastes and attention to curated detail that discerning homeowners prioritize when purchasing luxury properties.

The persona also resonates in premium consumer electronics, designer automobile, and bespoke jewelry or timepiece sales. Their elegant self-presentation personifies the artisanal craftsmanship and uncompromising quality emblematic of those marquee brands' exclusive cachet.

Any sales context where the perceived hallmarks of luxury, opulence, and prestige are the driving purchase influences will be a setting where the Cosmopolitan persona commands attention and exudes credibility. Their commitment to refinement is the product being bought and sold.

But Cosmopolitans might find it challenging to thrive in more casual or utilitarian industries that value practicality and a hands-on approach. Sales roles in industries like industrial equipment, agricultural products, or construction materials often require a more rugged and straightforward presentation.

The Cosmopolitan's emphasis on luxury and refinement may be perceived as overly extravagant or disconnected from the practical realities of those fields.

Remember: there is no right or wrong type of primary persona. Each persona comes with its unique set of strengths and challenges, whether you resonate with the unbounded spirit of the Explorer, the steadfast resolve of the Traditionalist, or the sophisticated flair of the Cosmopolitan.

If you resonate with the Explorer persona, your inherent approachability and adaptability are tremendous assets in industries such as outdoor equipment sales or educational services sales. Your relatability and hands-on approach can make sales experiences less intimidating and more enriching, bridging the gap between prospects or clients and the products or services they're exploring. But in leadership roles in more traditional settings, balancing the informal, adventurous spirit of the Explorer with the more conservative professional identity required can be difficult.

For the Traditionalist, your embodiment of trust and reliability lends itself well to fields such as insurance sales or government contracting sales where tradition and a steady approach are highly valued. Others are drawn to the stability you represent, creating an atmosphere where time-honored practices are appreciated.

The challenge may arise in industries that are rapidly innovating, such as media and entertainment sales, where there's a push for constant evolution and a risk of being seen as outdated.

The Cosmopolitan persona thrives in industries such as high-end fashion sales, global consulting services, or premium real estate sales where quality and a sophisticated professional identity are paramount. Your professional conduct suits leadership roles within these environments. But oftentimes the challenge is to balance this sophistication with genuine engagement to avoid being misread as aloof, especially in industries such as nonprofit fundraising or healthcare sales where a personal touch is crucial.

Yet, remember that your primary persona is the quintessence of your being, the inherent nature you carry from the cradle to the crescendo of your career. It's the unchanging core that defines your authentic self, and it's not something you should attempt to alter.

A Cosmopolitan attempting to mimic the Explorer's casual conduct, or an Explorer trying to copy the Traditionalist's formality often will feel as uncomfortable as when wearing an ill-fitting garment. This incongruence can radiate subtle cues of inauthenticity, leaving others with a sense of dissonance, even if they can't pinpoint what is causing it.

Instead, your adaptability comes from your secondary personas—the versatile facets of your identity that you've honed through experience, environment, and personal and professional development. Those are the aspects you can shift and shape to resonate with different individuals and situations.

Secondary personas enable you to purposefully imprint traits and characteristics onto others, facilitating instant connections without sacrificing the integrity of your true self. These are the facets of your identity that are more fluid, allowing for personal expression and change over time. The four secondary personas are not about changing who you are but about expanding the ways you can authentically interact with the world.

The Caregiver: Supportive and Nurturing

The style of Caregivers resonates with a delicate finesse. Caregivers are the sales professionals who thread warmth and nurturing into every interaction.

In their wardrobe you'll find fine patterns and soft fabrics that offer comfort, both to themselves and those they encounter. Soft colors, such as pastels, are prevalent, reflecting their gentle nature and contributing to a calming atmosphere wherever they go.

Caregivers curate a wardrobe that melds professional expectations with a personal touch. Shirts with delicate details, cardigans in soothing hues, and tailored slacks or skirts exemplify their effortless grace.

Their clothing is not merely a uniform but a testament to their role as a nurturer, blending the demands of their profession with innate compassion.

In their body image, Caregivers appreciate subtlety and health, finding beauty in the natural and the genuine. Their physical presence is characterized by an understated grace, maintaining a physique that speaks to vitality and genuine care rather than vanity.

For Caregivers, accessories and personal grooming are reflective of their tender approach to life. Jewelry is minimal and meaningful, shoes are chosen for comfort yet display quiet elegance or small embellishments, and grooming is consistent with their overall ethos—thoughtful and impeccably maintained.

When it comes to grooming, they approach it as they do their role, enhancing features softly and naturally, ensuring their presence is as reassuring as the support they offer. Their hair is often styled in a way that's practical yet inviting, perhaps a soft style or gentle waves, and their nails are kept clean and neatly groomed, often in muted or clear tones.

- **Keyword:** care
- **Perceived traits:** supportive, caring, warm, nurturing, considerate, compassionate, gentle, soft-spoken, receptive, demure
- **Perceived challenges:** anxious, emotional, dependent, insecure, noncompetitive, naïve, passive, undemanding, hesitant

The Caregiver finds its strongest calling in sales roles within industries that place a premium on empathetic personal guidance, emotional sensitivity, and a spirit of care and compassion.

Within healthcare sales—whether medical devices, pharmaceutical, nursing solutions, or patient care services—the Caregiver's nurturing nature is intrinsically credible. Veterinary care and pet product sales likewise allow the Caregiver's nurturing spirit to shine.

For industries like social work, counseling, community outreach, or nonprofit services, the Caregiver persona embodies the heartfelt investment and delicate handling those causes require.

This persona also resonates powerfully in education and training sales, from tutoring services to professional development programs.

In any sales context where emotional openness, personal and professional development, and care-centric culture are paramount, Caregivers provide an incomparably helpful guidance that makes them not just sales professionals but longstanding partners in their prospects' or clients' journeys.

But Caregivers might find it challenging to thrive in highly competitive and aggressive sales environments that prioritize hard-nosed negotiation and relentless pursuit of targets. Industries such as financial trading, corporate law services, or high-stakes real estate often require a more assertive and results-driven approach. The Caregiver's emphasis on empathy and nurturing may be perceived as a lack of competitiveness or decisiveness.

The Avant-Garde: Individualistic and Creative

The Avant-Garde stands as a testament to their creativity and self-expression, valuable in industries that prize innovation, such as interactive media sales, modern art sales, or forward-thinking technology sales industries. Their appearance is a vibrant tapestry of artistic exploration with a wardrobe that narrates stories of bold experimentation and the redefining of boundaries.

They select audacious colors, embrace emerging designers, and favor unique silhouettes that are the hallmarks of their style, a visual celebration of their commitment to pushing the frontiers of fashion. The maintenance of their wardrobe is an act of artistic devotion, each piece cared for with precision or, sometimes, creatively repurposed in their ongoing narrative.

The Avant-Garde views their physique as a medium for artistic display, embracing a spectrum of styles that challenge conventional beauty norms. They wear their confidence as effortlessly as their eclectic mix of garments, radiating a presence that commands attention and sparks dialogue. They approach their health with an artistic flair, aligning their physical activities and mental wellness practices with their creative life, even if it means deviating from conventional health routines.

Their accessories, from their statement jewelry to their sculptural shoes, are not mere embellishments but proclamations of their originality, each chosen for its unique design and the conversation it incites.

Their grooming routines are an extension of their creative ethos. Grooming is an opportunity for innovation, and hair and nail care become expressions of their Avant-Garde identity, transcending the typical to become part of their artistic statement. Every element of their appearance is a deliberate choice, a chapter in the creative odyssey they embody, inviting all to witness the living art they present to the world.

- **Keyword:** creativity
- **Perceived traits:** innovative, imaginative, free-spirited, independent, original, unique, unconventional, fearless, impromptu
- **Perceived challenges:** unrealistic, undisciplined, opinionated, neglectful, inconsistent, disruptive, contrary, awkward

The Avant-Garde's unconventional creativity finds its ideal expression in sales arenas that celebrate bold visionaries and innovative artistic leadership. Creative agencies, cutting-edge tech, entertainment, and the arts are their playgrounds.

Within advertising, marketing, and branding agencies the Avant-Garde persona embodies the pioneering philosophies and boundary-defying ethos those industries prize.

Their artistic self-expression and nonconformist persona aligns with the expectation to deliver disruptive, creative solutions.

They shine equally bright as brand ambassadors for forward-thinking technology companies engaged in AI, web3, immersive realities, and other future-shaping products and services. The Avant-Garde essence captivates early adopters hungry for visionary ideas that expand possibilities.

Entertainment sales roles across music, film, TV, live events, and cultural experiences allow the Avant-Garde to embody the artistic energy driving those creative works.

Similarly, in galleries, museums, and modern or contemporary art sales, the Avant-Garde is uniquely equipped to convey transcendent appreciation for groundbreaking, creative movements.

Any sales context celebrating creativity without limits, inspired innovation, and design-forward futurism provides an ideal stage for the Avant-Garde persona to shine at their genre-defying best.

But Avant-Gardes might find it challenging to thrive in highly regulated or traditional industries that prioritize conformity and adherence to established norms.

Sales roles in industries like pharmaceuticals, corporate finance, or government contracting often require a more conventional and disciplined approach. The Avant-Garde's emphasis on creativity and nonconformity may be perceived as disruptive or unprofessional.

The Glamorous: Magnetic and Extravagant

The Glamorous persona is a paragon of attention and fashion, making them a natural fit for industries such as luxury goods sales, high-end event sales, or entertainment sales public relations. Their wardrobe is a bastion of opulence, each piece resonating with the allure of a meticulously curated collection. Picture them in attire that captivates with its shimmering details, reflective finishes, and bold color palette, from the fierceness of reds to the solemnity of blacks and the nobility of purples.

When it comes to maintaining their wardrobe, they exercise some care in trying to preserve each piece as a cherished element of their sumptuous attire. But if that doesn't work, no worries; they'll just move on to the next fashion item.

They regard their body as integral to their personal identity; they sculpt their physique to harmonize with their taste and social stature. Their fitness routines are as much a part of their brand narrative as their choice of wardrobe, enhancing their aesthetic and their presence.

Their accessories are selected for their storytelling power and their ability to accentuate their captivating presence. But these pieces don't have to be luxurious jewelry or high-end designer shoes. What matters more than the price tag is how much attention the piece can draw to their look.

Their grooming routines are conducted with the same precision and intentionality as dressing for a gala. For them, grooming is artistry, hair care is a discipline, and skin care is a devotion, each facet executed to radiate charisma and draw admiration.

This scrupulous cultivation of their appearance reflects a profound appreciation for the transformative power of appearance.

- **Keyword:** attraction
- **Perceived traits:** trendy, stimulating, popular, magnetic, fit, extravagant, daring, attractive, admirable
- **Perceived challenges:** pompous, one-dimensional, manipulative, insincere, indiscreet, flamboyant, deceitful, artificial

The Glamorous persona shines in sales arenas centered around fashion, beauty, entertainment, and overall cultivation of magnetic personal presence. Their extravagant essence aligns almost perfectly with image-driven businesses.

Within the fashion and apparel industry, the Glamorous energy is tailormade for representing designer brands, premium clothing lines, and aspirational accessory makers.

The commitment of the Glamorous to alluring self-presentation complements the transformative escape those products provide for prospects or clients.

This persona finds an equally compelling fit in the world of beauty, cosmetics, and personal care product sales. The Glamorous' dedication to personal branding reinforces the self-indulgent luxury and empowered radiance those offerings enable.

For roles in public relations, communications, and personal branding consultancies, the Glamorous persona's pure magnetism makes them ideal ambassadors.

The entertainment universe provides a sumptuous stage for the Glamorous as well, whether representing fashion houses partnering with film or TV, handling celebrity influencer relations, or managing talent for musicians and live performers. Their tantalizing showmanship personifies the rarefied glamour of those worlds.

Similarly, within television, radio, live events, and brand activations centered on aspirational popular culture, the Glamorous essence conveys the irresistible spectacle and grandeur prospects and clients envision.

Any sales context where magnetic attraction, self-actualized confidence, and uncompromising cultivation of enviable personal image are paramount will be a stage waiting for the Glamorous persona's spellbinding radiance to captivate.

But the Glamorous might find it challenging to thrive in industries that prioritize practicality, minimalism, or a subdued professional identity. Sales roles in businesses such as industrial equipment, agricultural products, or technical consulting often require a more straightforward and utilitarian approach. The Glamorous persona's emphasis on extravagance and attention-grabbing aesthetics may be perceived as excessive or out of place.

The Dramatic: Strong and Fearless

The Dramatic persona has an unforgettable presence, embodying a love for the bold that can be harnessed in roles from creative sales directorships to performance art sales management. Their wardrobe is an audacious array of statement pieces that seize attention, mirroring the boldness of their personality.

Their wardrobe is a testament to their fearlessness with each item chosen for its impact. Theirs is a fashion that doesn't simply capture the limelight, it generates it, ensuring Dramatic personas aren't merely observed but remembered. Architectural collars, oversized sleeves, and other unconventional silhouettes are their staples, each piece a statement in itself.

They revel in the strength and sophistication of black, black, and more black, allowing it to dominate their wardrobe as the color of their joy. When they opt for another color, it's strategically employed to forge a stark, memorable contrast that complements their daring sartorial narrative.

The maintenance of their wardrobe is as exacting and dramatic as a theater's costume shop—detailed, intentional, and always in pursuit of the remarkable.

They view their body as a stage for a commanding performance. Their confidence is their most treasured garment, enveloping a physique that is as dynamic as their sartorial choices, making a statement as memorable as their own dramatic essence.

Their accessories and grooming routines are essential to their expressive arsenal. Each piece of jewelry, every selection of shoes, and every grooming choice is a thoughtful act of self-expression, adding bold lines to the story they embody.

For the Dramatic, the world is a vast stage, and they are always in the lead role with each facet of their appearance carefully curated to etch a lasting impression of their indelible presence in any professional setting.

- **Keyword:** power
- **Perceived traits:** strong, intense, charismatic, demanding, bold, commanding, captivating, aloof, severe, spectacular
- **Perceived challenges:** tough, possessive, intrusive, intense, insensitive, harsh, dominating, cold

Within the performing arts—whether theatre, dance, music, or other live entertainment—Dramatics shine as promoters, venue directors, and production company sales leads.

The fashion industry provides another dynamic runway for Dramatic merchandise and apparel brand managers. Their authoritative persona advocates for the unbridled creativity and daring visions driving those statement-making collections.

As account directors for advertising agencies, marketing firms, and brand consultancies, they orchestrate the corporate narratives and breakthrough campaigns their clients crave. Their persuasive charisma personifies those creative concepts.

For digital media like streaming video, podcasts, or innovative content platforms, Dramatic on-air personalities, show-runners, and subscription sales leadership roles allow their impassioned storytelling abilities to shine.

And within the luxury goods stratosphere, Dramatics personify the uncompromising decadence of premium brands, shaping the elite client experiences around haute couture, jewelry, collectibles, and other rarified indulgences.

Any sales context where entrancing persuasion, gravitational personal presence, and amplified self-assuredness are competitive differentiators provides the main stage the Dramatic persona yearns to command.

But Dramatics might find it challenging to thrive in industries that emphasize subtlety, modesty, and a collaborative approach over individual showmanship. Sales roles in industries such as healthcare, educational services, or government relations often require more subdued and team-oriented conduct. The Dramatic persona's emphasis on boldness and theatricality may be perceived as overbearing or distracting.

It's your secondary persona that allows you to adapt to various roles and environments. Balancing these secondary personas is key to meeting diverse expectations while staying true to your core values. Although balance is crucial, it's important to note that misperceptions often arise when sales leaders lean too heavily into the extremes of these personas.

Take the Caregiver, for example. Although the characteristics of empathy, attentiveness, and warmth are crucial traits required for impactful sales leadership, solely embodying this secondary persona in extremes can lead others to perceive only the caregiver within you. This can overshadow the fact that you also possess qualities such as assertiveness or strategic thinking that might come from your primary persona. These are the sales professionals who enter meetings in flowing attire with overly casual hairstyles and impractical shoes.

They're the first to organize treats for the gathering and ask about everyone's personal lives in a soft-spoken voice. They prioritize harmony in teams and may hesitate to speak up. As a result, they might face the harsh reality of being stereotyped solely as Caregivers, which would overlook their multifaceted abilities. And although the Caregiver is an outstanding persona, it's the one that many sales professionals automatically get pigeonholed into based on their stereotyped roles as nurturers and caretakers.

Or consider an Avant-Garde and their inherent creativity and self-expression, which is often seen as bold and boundary-pushing. Their daring nature and unconventional approach make them excellent conduits for embodying traits such as innovation and risk-taking. But when your behavior, your communication, and even your visual appearance veer too far into this secondary persona, it can lead to misperceptions.

These are the sales professionals who may prioritize bold fashion choices, unconventional hairstyles, or extensive grooming routines in professional settings. They're the ones with sticky notes covering their screens and markers coloring their notebooks, the ones who constantly disrupt meetings with out-of-the-box thinking, sometimes neglecting practicality and execution. Although these traits can be empowering and impactful in certain contexts, being exclusively identified with the Avant-Garde persona might overshadow other valuable aspects of their primary persona, potentially limiting opportunities for recognition and advancement.

Or there's the Glamorous, the one we admire for their style, the shine they bring into every encounter, the fashion runway they walk all day long. Yet, if these sales professionals go too far, they risk being perceived solely for their outer appearance, overshadowing their intelligence, dedication, and hard work. These are the sales leaders who may overdo it with their hair, grooming, and attire, opting for excessive glamour, glitter, and skin exposure. Their ensembles may prioritize style over substance, leading to misperceptions for others to discover the smart, dedicated, hard-working sales leader under the glamorous exterior.

And last we have the Dramatic personas, captivating and commanding attention wherever they go. Although outstanding in situations where a dramatic nature is required, such as on stage or in public communication, when taken to extremes, they risk overshadowing others and being perceived as intimidating or trying too hard. Their powerful behavior and communication style, although effective in some contexts, can come off as cold or competitive, hindering collaboration and rapport-building efforts. It's essential for them to strike a balance, harnessing their dramatic flair when appropriate while remaining approachable and being considerate of others' contributions and perspectives.

As you can see, there is no perfect persona. There's no good or bad; you are uniquely you, and that's who you should be.

But it's often when we allow our secondary personas to dominate that they overshadow our true essence, our primary personas. It's about finding harmony and balance within ourselves and embracing all facets of our identity while ensuring that none overshadow the core of who we are. It's about contextually curating your expression to meet the moment and enhancing your authentic self without losing your essence.

As you continue on your journey, let this understanding guide you. Embrace your primary persona as well as the qualities of your secondary persona to navigate the myriad of expectations you encounter in your own unique and authentic way.

And should you seek to delve deeper into the fabric of your perceived identity, the end of this book provides a gateway. There you will find a QR code and a link to a perception persona audit available on my website, a free tool designed to offer insights into which primary or secondary persona you are currently embodying or are perceived to be.

Chapter 5
Leaders Look Professional

**Strategic Moves to Authority:
Positioning for the End Game.**

Chapter 5:
Leaders Look Professional

Navigating the shifting sands of what defines "professional" in today's workplace is an intricate dance, particularly for sales professionals. The archetype of professional attire has transcended the era when a crisp suit and conservative accessories demarcated the threshold of leadership and ambition. Today, the concept of looking professional for sales leaders is a vibrant tapestry, mirroring the vast expanse of industries from corporate to nonprofit to education to entrepreneurship and reflecting diverse cultures, generations, and personal styles.

In the past, dress code levels were the compass that directed professional attire for sales professionals. Those sartorial standards were not just about fashion; they were emblems of seriousness, competence, and intent within a professional context. They also allowed (and still allow) organizations to create a sense of unity and professionalism through a shared visual standard.

From the finesse of boardroom attire to the ease of casual wear, those guidelines established by dress codes provided a narrative for professional presentation. Once the silent custodians of a professional's wardrobe, dress codes have become historical markers from which the present-day dynamic fashion ethos has emerged.

Let's briefly revisit those dress codes, not as the definitive rule book they once were, but as a history lesson from which today's fluid fashion landscape has evolved.

Dress code level one: boardroom attire. Boardroom attire was the pinnacle of professional wear, encapsulating formality. Sales professionals adorned themselves with classic suits in dark, commanding hues that were paired with pristine white dress shirts. Skirts for women maintained a knee-length standard, and their accessories were selected for subtlety—closed-toe dress shoes with pantyhose as an indispensable companion, irrespective of the season, and jewelry that whispered of status, such as understated watches or cufflinks. Hair was often styled in a restrained manner, and makeup was applied with a light hand to accentuate a look of natural authority.

Dress code level two: traditional business attire. Traditional business attire offered a broader palette and softer lines. Suits branched into lighter colors and subtle patterns while dress shirts could bring a pop of color or a delicate print. Skirts for women relaxed slightly in fit, and footwear expanded to include colored dress shoes. Accessories, such as ties or scarves, could introduce a personal touch, and jewelry might make a bolder statement. Hairstyles softened, and makeup could venture beyond the bare essentials to enhance confidence and presence.

Dress code level three: executive casual. Executive casual introduced an even more personal touch. Blazers paired with slacks or skirts provided a blend of authority and approachability, and the use of fabric and color became more diverse. Dress shoes remained the standard, and hair and makeup could echo the wearer's personality, offering a palette for more vivid expression. More pronounced accessories allowed creativity to shine through.

Dress code level four: mainstream casual. Mainstream casual offered a departure from tradition. Dress shirts gave way to more relaxed button-downs, even embracing short sleeves for a touch of informality. The color spectrum widened, and patterns became more playful.

Footwear could be comfortably chic, reflecting personal style and practicality. Accessories served as a focal point for individuality, and hair could be more freely styled. Makeup for women, in harmony with this casual air, could be more experimental.

Dress code level five: baseline casual. Baseline casual was the embodiment of relaxed professionalism. Denim could be polished enough for a casual work setting, provided it was clean and well-fitted. Tops could be comfortable yet remain tasteful, and shoes could range from loafers to tasteful sneakers, as long as they were well-kept. Hair could be worn in a variety of styles that still conveyed intentionality, and makeup for women could be as understated or as expressive as the overall ensemble allowed. Accessories, although still present, were chosen for comfort and personal expression.

But let's pause for a moment and consider the present. The rules that once dictated professional appearance have been blurred by the evolving landscape of the modern workplace. The once rigid frameworks have softened, morphing into a more nuanced spectrum of acceptable workwear.

The concept of "casual" is nebulous and subjective: The transition toward a more casual wardrobe in many workplaces has introduced a new challenge. Whereas the traditional business dress code was meticulously defined, the concept of "casual" remains nebulous and subjective. This issue often leads to uncertainty and inconsistency, as what one person considers business casual might be seen as too informal by another. This ambiguity requires sales leaders to develop a keen sense of appropriateness, balancing comfort with professionalism.

Cultural diversity reshapes dress norms: The integration of diverse cultural norms into the workplace adds another layer of complexity to defining professional or casual dress.

With each culture comes a distinct perspective on what constitutes appropriate, which can vary significantly. What is considered respectful in one culture might be seen as too formal or too casual in another. This diversity necessitates a more inclusive and understanding approach to dress codes, recognizing and respecting a wide range of cultural expressions.

Generational views create dress code challenges: The generational mosaic present in today's workforce further complicates matters. Each generation brings its own set of attitudes toward self-expression and conformity. Older generations might prefer more traditional business attire, while younger generations often lean toward a more relaxed and individualistic style. Navigating these generational preferences requires a flexible approach that honors the values of all employees.

Emphasis on diversity, equity, and inclusion reshapes dress codes: As organizations place greater emphasis on creating diverse, equitable, and inclusive workplaces, there has been a recognition that traditional dress codes can be exclusionary or discriminatory. This reality has led to a more flexible, inclusive approach to workwear policies, ensuring that all employees can express their identities without fear of prejudice.

Typical gender expression is no longer confined to binary norms: Gender expression has morphed, challenging traditional dress norms even further. The binary understanding of gender-specific clothing is giving way to a more inclusive perspective. This evolution is reflected in the acceptance of diverse gender expressions through fashion, allowing individuals to dress in ways that align with their true selves rather than conforming to norms.

The internet blurs fashion lines: The influence of social media and the internet has democratized fashion and trendsetting, often further blurring the lines between personal and professional attire. Trends that start online will quickly make their way into the office, challenging traditional notions of workplace appropriateness.

Remote work fosters informality: The pandemic has undeniably reshaped our perceptions of professional attire. The shift to remote work and the adoption of screen-to-screen interactions have introduced a level of informality previously unseen in many industries, blurring the lines between home and office.

Work-life boundaries are increasingly blurred: With the rise of flexible working arrangements, the gig economy, and the "always-on" nature of modern work, the boundaries between work and personal life have become increasingly blurred. These changes have contributed to a more fluid approach to workwear as professionals seek to integrate their personal style with their professional identity. The need to be ready for both a video conference and a quick errand outside means that workwear must be versatile and comfortable yet still presentable.

Customer interactions now demand authenticity: In many industries there has been a shift toward more personalized interactions with prospects or clients. This has led to a questioning of the traditional "suited and booted" approach to sales. The idea is that a more authentic, relatable appearance can help build trust and rapport with prospects or clients. Sales leaders must now consider how their appearance can reflect their genuine personality and foster a sense of connection rather than simply adhering to outdated standards of professionalism.

These factors, combined with the rise of individualism, suggest that the future of attire in the workplace will continue to evolve, prioritizing adaptability and personal expression alongside traditional notions of professionalism.

The challenge for today's sales leaders is to navigate this ever-changing landscape and to set a standard that balances personal authenticity with the expectations of their professional roles. Professional attire should honor the gravitas of their fields yet be adaptable enough to navigate the modern world's demands.

It's about finding that common visual language that respects the tradition of their professions while welcoming the individuality each professional brings to their role.

As we have moved beyond the rigidity of traditional dress code levels, the contemporary professional landscape doesn't offer a one-size-fits-all prescription that can encompass the myriad of factors influencing a sales professional's choice of dress in the workplace. The modern sales leader's wardrobe is less about conforming to strict rules and more about crafting a personal dress code that, in the best case, performs the following functions:

- **Bolsters their confidence,** making them feel invincible and authentic in their skin, ready to tackle any challenge with the poise of a superhero.

- **Respects the environment in which they operate,** whether it's the industry nuances, the cultural ethos of their organization, or the expectations tied to their role.

- **Considers the audience they will encounter,** dressing not just for the position they hold but also for the individuals they serve and collaborate with.

- **Facilitates versatility,** embracing an array of settings and occasions. It's about selecting pieces to be mixed and matched for any engagement or unexpected encounter.

- **Demonstrates deliberate choices,** showing their attire is a thoughtful component of their professional tool kit.

- **Pays attention to details,** recognizing that grooming, accessories, or the right finishing touches are the final steps to an intentional look.

- **Invests in quality over quantity**, understanding that well-crafted garments are a testament to their professionalism and the capability to invest in themselves.

- **Balances current trends with classic staples**, ensuring their wardrobe remains relevant yet timeless.

- **Knows the narrative it wants to express**, understanding that each garment reflects a chapter of their personal identity story, thus aligning their external presentation with their internal values and goals.

- **Complements rather than overshadows** their intrinsic talents and abilities, using fashion to accentuate their strengths without causing unnecessary distraction.

- **Allows their presence to take center stage** with a look that doesn't clamor for attention but supports their professional identity.

- **Avoids the pitfall of feeling compelled to mirror** traditionally gendered dress expectations, asserting that authority are not monopolized by any gender identity.

- **Eschews the pressure to conform to gender norms**, reinforcing the idea that their value is not predicated on these norms but on their expertise and contributions.

- **Embraces trial and error** as part of the refinement process, experimenting with new looks and evolving their personal dress code based on feedback and self-reflection.

And last, but most important, let's reconceptualize a familiar maxim: "Dress for the job you want, not the one you have." Although this adage has merit, I propose a broader perspective: "Dress not just for the next rung on the career ladder but with your ultimate objective in mind."

Envision the pinnacle of your career—perhaps it's to become the Chief Revenue Officer of a leading organization, an influential industry expert, or an innovator in your field. Whatever your goal, it's vital to begin embodying that role now.

Your wardrobe should be a reflection of your ambition and a projection of your potential. It's about more than the clothes you wear; it's about a consistent expression of your professional identity that aligns with the zenith of your aspirations. Each day is an opportunity to illustrate not just where you are or where you want to be next, but where you are determined to be.

Prescribed Uniformity in Action

In many professions, uniforms are the silent ambassadors of the organization, immediately recognizable symbols that communicate volumes without a word being spoken. They serve as a bridge of trust and authority between the role they have, the person wearing them, and those they serve. Legal and ethical codes are also interwoven into the very fabric of these uniforms, ensuring they adhere to stringent industry standards and safety protocols. They reflect a commitment to upholding the highest professional benchmarks of the field.

In law enforcement, individuals adorned with badges stand as stalwarts of justice and order, embodying the law's might and the community's trust. The law enforcement uniform symbolizes a bastion of safety intended to instantly command respect and project the power vested in those who have taken on those roles.

In military service, the distinct camouflage or dress uniforms worn by service members signify honor and discipline. The precise insignia, medals, and ribbons communicate rank, experience, and dedication to service, reflecting an unyielding allegiance to national defense and the collective ethos of their units.

The healthcare industry embraces uniforms as a symbol of cleanliness and precision. Whether it's the scrubs of a surgical team or the white coats of doctors, the garments communicate a commitment to care and a readiness to heal. Healthcare uniforms represent a shared identity rooted in expertise and empathy, central to the healer's covenant with patients and colleagues alike.

Pilots and flight crew in the airline industry wear uniforms that reflect precision and professionalism and that are designed to instill confidence in travelers. A pilot's crisp uniform signifies not just their ability to navigate the skies but also their leadership in ensuring passengers' safety and comfort.

On the manufacturing floor, the uniform serves a dual purpose: it is both protective gear and an emblem of the collective industrial effort. Leaders in manufacturing often wear uniforms that resonate with the workforce's attire while distinguishing their supervisory status, signaling an alignment with the production heart of the industry while steering its operations.

These uniforms—be they adorned with stripes, badges, or safety gear—are not simply mandatory attire. They are potent symbols of the roles individuals have carved out in industries that are often physically demanding and require decisive leadership. Such uniforms bridge the gap between individual capability and collective identity, asserting a visual dialogue of expertise and empowerment.

But uniforms are not reserved for traditional uniformed services, they still play a crucial role in some sales environments. These standardized attires serve as powerful visual ambassadors, aligning the sales team with the brand's identity.

In the automotive sales industry, it's common for sales professionals at dealerships to wear polo shirts, blazers, or full automotive uniforms branded with the dealership's logo that represents the vehicle brands they sell.

Similarly, sales teams at major retail chains like department stores, big box stores, or consumer electronics retailers often wear colored smocks, vests, or lanyards with company branding as part of their required uniform. It signals their sales role to shoppers.

Those in door-to-door sales or direct sales roles representing particular product lines like food storage, cosmetics, or cleaning supplies often have a uniform consisting of branded polo shirts and, sometimes, full outfits with logo insignias that identify them while canvassing neighborhoods.

A branded uniform doesn't just identify sales professionals, it presents them as walking advertisements for their organization, solidifying their role as an official ambassador for that brand's identity and service standards.

When people wear a uniform they take on a mantle of responsibility and an equalizer that underscores their role within a larger team and organization. A uniform is much more than fabric and thread—it's a declaration of commitment.

The relationship between a uniform and the person wearing it is both intimate and open. It can kindle a sense of belonging and purpose, creating an instant visual connection with the public. The uniform is thoughtfully designed to marry necessity with dignity while allowing the wearer to perform their duties with competence and confidence. A uniform accounts for the rigorous demands of the role and the physical needs of the wearer, including practicality, comfort, and safety.

In environments where uniforms are the norm, the scope for personal expression may seem limited, but individuals can still find creative avenues to infuse their look of leadership. Small, compliant changes can help add a personal touch. Sometimes the choice of accessories, while remaining within the parameters set by the profession, allows for subtle distinctions. The flair of a tasteful pin or the understated elegance of a classic watch can speak to a person's personal style without detracting from the uniformity required. A patterned tie or a functional yet stylish belt could be a signifier of identity. Where regulations allow, a slight variation in footwear or the style or color of socks could add a discreet touch of personality. In addition, hair accessories used to secure styles can be both practical and a reflection of personal taste. Even a modest name tag or badge with a distinctive font or style can serve as a hallmark of individuality, transforming a generic item into something personal and unique.

These choices, although seemingly minor, can have an impact on how individuals are perceived and, more importantly, how they perceive themselves within their roles.

Moreover, the meticulous care of the uniform itself—the sharpness of a crease, the precision of a tuck, the cleanliness and crispness of the fabric—can convey a professional's dedication to their role and attention to detail. It is in these meticulously maintained details that individual pride and professionalism shine.

Silent Standards and Unwritten Uniforms

If you think the dialogue on uniforms doesn't apply to your field, perhaps you should think again. Every industry, every organization, and every role operates within a set of unspoken expectations—silent standards that compose the unwritten uniform of the professional world. These are not codified in employee handbooks, yet they exist in the collective consciousness, guiding impressions from boardrooms to open-plan offices.

In the world of financial services, for instance, even without a formal mandate, the uniform might include conservative suits, crisp shirts, and subtle accessories.

Or consider a tech start-up where hoodies, T-shirts, and jeans have become the emblematic garb of innovation and disruptive thinking.

In creative industries such as advertising and design, there's an expectation to embody creativity, not just in work but also in appearance. Here, eclectic attire and bold color choices are often the norm, signaling a creative mind at work.

Moving into the public industry, educators are expected to strike a balance between approachable and authoritative, often opting for smart casual attire that encourages respect while being relatable to students.

Nonprofit leaders might adopt an approach that blends professionalism with the grassroots essence of their work, often choosing functional and practical clothing that resonates with their mission and the communities they serve.

Whether selling consumer packaged goods to stores or representing a major retail brand, the unspoken expectation is a refined, accessible look aligned with the target consumer—professional yet approachable attire that appeals to mainstream tastes.

In industries like fine jewelry, fashion, high-end automotive, or premium real estate, projecting affluence and sophistication is critical. The unspoken uniform borders on "runway luxury," reflecting the opulent lifestyles those products embody.

The unifying thread is that each unspoken uniform aims to personify the professional archetypes and establish a tribal signaling system that prospects, clients, and colleagues can read at a glance, separating the true representatives from the imposters.

By decoding these silent standards, sales leaders can navigate their industries with a more nuanced understanding of unarticulated yet powerful norms. It's about reading the room, understanding the culture, and dressing in a way that communicates that you belong, that you are a credible player in the field, and that you respect the unspoken rules of the game. But how can you define what your silent uniform should look like?

First, look around. It's as simple as that. Is there a pattern in the way professionals dress in your workplace or industry? It's not about mimicking or conforming blindly but about understanding the visual language and nuances. Take note of the colors, the fits, the levels of formality. Observe the details: the watches, the shoes, the way a tie is knotted, or how a blazer is buttoned. These subtleties are your clues.

Consider the context of your interactions. In client meetings, is there a dominant style? At networking events, what styles stand out and seem to align with success and influence? These are your guideposts. From the boardroom to casual Fridays, each setting has its unwritten dress code that, once deciphered, can be tailored to your advantage.

Reflect on your role within the organization. What are the expectations, spoken and unspoken, for someone in your position? How can your look of leadership showcase your professional strengths and personality without you speaking a word? Remember: your silent uniform is not just about fitting in, it's about standing out in the right ways. It's about aligning your external presentation with your career aspirations and the persona you want to project.

Define how far you can integrate your personal touch. Once you understand the silent standards, you can start bending them subtly. It's about finding the balance between industry expectations and your personal style, the sweet spot where your silent uniform empowers you to feel authentic and confident in your professional skin.

Then go back to our preceding exploration of perception personas when we unveiled the power of keywords—comfort, values, quality, care, creativity, attraction, and power—that anchor the essence of our professional identities. You might see that your unwritten uniform speaks to those keywords and the perceived traits they represent. Silent uniforms are not decreed by policy but are ingrained in the fabric of industry expectations and professional culture.

Does this mean you need to overhaul your wardrobe and change your perception persona to fully match the uniform your industry, corporate culture, or profession expect? No, not at all.

But coming to an understanding might elucidate why, in certain contexts, you feel like a seamless part of the tapestry, whereas in others you feel like you stand out without being able to pinpoint the reason. It's not about altering your core identity; it's about fine-tuning the following characteristics:

Balancing personas: Everyone has a primary persona and one or more secondary personas. It's about leveraging this spectrum appropriately. For instance, your Caregiver qualities may be front and center in a nurturing role, whereas your secondary Avant-Garde traits can come into play when innovation is called for. Balancing personas is about the strategic interplay between different facets of your character. It recognizes that a sales leader is not one-dimensional. You can be nurturing and innovative, methodical and creative all at once. By emphasizing certain traits in specific contexts, you can align your professional identity with your role's expectations while maintaining your unique essence. This alignment enhances your relatability and effectiveness, allowing you to connect with others on multiple levels and in a variety of scenarios.

Borrowing elements: This is about selectively adopting characteristics from other personas that resonate with your personal style. A Glamorous persona might borrow small elements from the Cosmopolitan's flair for quality for a high-stakes business meeting, or a Traditionalist could take on a nuance from the Caregiver's warm approach for a team-building retreat. Borrowing elements involves curating aspects from other personas to complement your own dominant traits. This selective synthesis creates a dynamic professional identity that can adapt and thrive across a range of settings. It's about enriching your personal narrative by integrating diverse qualities that broaden your appeal and enhance your influence. This nuanced approach enables you to be perceived as multifaceted and versatile, showcasing your ability to evolve and respond to a variety of professional challenges.

Certainly, you also can choose to disrupt these patterns of unspoken uniforms. History is punctuated with stories of leaders who have shattered expectations and redefined the norms of their industries, becoming icons of success on their own terms and with their own looks. They are trailblazers, the rare exceptions who prove that rules can be broken with the right combination of timing, talent, and tenacity.

Yet, it is crucial to acknowledge that these cases are exceptional for a reason—they stand out against a backdrop of more typical narratives. For every convention-defying success story, there are countless others who navigate the intricate dance of expectations and self-expression with more subtlety. The most common pathway to success often involves aligning with the established norms while finding small but significant ways to showcase individuality.

The decision, ultimately, is deeply personal. It's about weighing the potential benefits of fully disrupting the existing norm or standing out step-by-step. It's about understanding not just who you are but how best to convey that identity in a way that resonates within your professional context. This is not about surrendering to the status quo but about making informed choices.

Your career, your professional identity, your persona, your style—these are yours to define. Whether you choose to align with silent standards or set your own course, your look of leadership can be a powerful tool in your professional arsenal. Use it with purpose, with insight and, most important, with a clear vision of the outcome you desire. The silent uniform of your industry or role doesn't need to be a straitjacket; it can be a canvas—sometimes for blending in, sometimes for standing out. The art is in knowing when to do which, and the wisdom is in recognizing the choice is always, unequivocally, yours.

Internal Mandates We Self-Enforce

Yes, you read that right. Many of us are guilty of setting unwritten rules for ourselves, internal guidelines we adhere to—often unconsciously—that shape our professional identity. These self-imposed standards can be as binding as any corporate dress code, yet they stem not from a company policy but from our own insecurities and the societal expectations we've absorbed.

This self-enforcement can manifest in numerous ways, subtly dictating our choices. It's the invisible uniform we design for ourselves, woven from the threads of the "shoulds" and "musts" we've collected throughout our professional lives. They are the mental garments made up of beliefs about how we need to appear to be accepted, respected, and successful. It's time to take a closer look at the expectations some of us have built for ourselves:

Conforming to traditionally masculine dress codes is a notion deeply rooted in the historical context of the workplace. For decades, power and authority have been visually represented by masculine attire—sharp suits, strict silhouettes, and muted colors. As women entered male-dominated fields, the prevailing belief was that, to succeed, women would have to assimilate, often meaning mirroring the look of their male counterparts. But that approach is outdated and not recommended.

First, it can suppress your unique identity, compelling you to fit into an aesthetic that may not resonate with your personal style or the full breadth of your professional capabilities. If traditionally masculine attire feels inauthentic to you, it can affect your confidence and performance. Remember: your clothing is not just fabric; it's psychological armor. When you dress in ways that make you feel strong and genuine, your mindset and actions tend to match that authenticity. Second, this notion might unintentionally uphold the very gender biases that many industries are striving to overcome. This notion implies that, to be a leader, you must downplay attributes that aren't traditionally masculine. Equating a masculine appearance with professionalism risks negating the diverse ways in which individuals can express their professional identity.

Instead, choose a look that reflects your professional identity and personal style, allowing a richer expression of leadership. This is not about clothes overshadowing capability; it's about reinforcing that authority and professionalism are defined by your actions and knowledge, not the cut or color of your clothing.

Dressing in an overly gendered manner to emphasize gender identity can be a nuanced issue within the professional world. The inclination to overaccentuate gender with decidedly ornate clothing or exceptionally elaborate grooming routines might stem from a desire to assert your identity in a workplace that traditionally hasn't recognized gender diversity. It can be an attempt to reclaim the narrative of gender expression in spaces where it has been undervalued or overlooked.

But just as adopting a predominantly masculine wardrobe can have pitfalls, so too can an excessively gendered presentation. It risks diverting attention from your competence to your appearance, overshadowing your professional expertise with personal aesthetics. The silent but potent subtext is that your professional value is intertwined with conventional beauty standards, potentially undermining the respect you command based on merit and accomplishments.

While there's power in embracing and expressing your gender identity, it's crucial to find a balance. The key is striking a harmonious chord between asserting your gender identity and underscoring your professional identity. Your goal should be to be acknowledged for your leadership acumen and contributions, not solely for the gender you express through your wardrobe or grooming choices.

Prioritizing others' needs over your own often goes hand-in-hand with minimizing attention on yourself. This self-enforced austerity can emerge from a place of nurturing that places the needs of family, colleagues, your community, or your role above your own. While it reflects commendable selflessness, it can inadvertently lead to self-neglect. You may find yourself allocating resources—time, money, and energy—to support and uplift others, even if it means your professional wardrobe takes a backseat. But this can result in a professional identity that doesn't reflect your status or ambition, possibly affecting how you're perceived.

There's a fine line between being resourceful and neglecting or underselling yourself.

Consistently limiting your expenditure on yourself might unwittingly signal that you don't value yourself or your role as much as you should. Although fiscal prudence is a virtue, it's also important to recognize that investing in your professional identity is not mere vanity, it's an integral part of your positing.

The goal is to achieve a balance where caring for others doesn't come at the expense of neglecting your needs. Recognize that you can be a supportive leader while still honoring your personal and professional requirements. Allow yourself permission to invest in your professional identity to feel confident and capable, reflecting the leader you truly are.

Holding on to the belief that what has worked for years will continue to serve you well can be another pitfall, especially regarding your wardrobe. For you, it might reinforce a mindset that undervalues your personal and professional progress and self-worth, potentially leading to stagnation in both self-image and career development.

Others might perceive an unchanging appearance as a reluctance to adapt to new career phases or as a lack of investment in your professional growth. In the workplace, where visual cues often communicate ambition and dynamism, an unaltered look could mistakenly signal complacency or lack of innovation.

This isn't about chasing every fleeting trend or dismissing the value of timeless statement pieces. But when years turn into a decade with the same look, it may be time to acknowledge that your sartorial choices need to be updated. Periodically adapting your professional attire signals to colleagues and external partners alike that you are evolving, attuned to the present, and investing in your career journey.

Updating your look of leadership isn't frivolity; it's a strategic refresh, signaling your continued relevance and evolution in your career and beyond.

Struggling with an "age-appropriate" look is a tug-of-war that spans the spectrum of most professionals' lives. As a leader, you might wrestle with the expectation of dressing in a way that aligns with perceived age norms—being trendy and youthful or reserved and mature. This self-imposed standard can be confining, often leading to a wardrobe that feels out of sync with your personal identity and professional acumen.

Younger professionals may feel the need to dress older to garner respect and authority, whereas older professionals might feel the need to dress younger to maintain a veneer of vitality and relevance. This pendulum swing between dressing older or younger to meet external expectations underscores a deeper issue—conformity to age norms as a perceived prerequisite for professional acceptance.

The challenge lies in transcending these societal dictates that attempt to define what is suitable for various ages within professional contexts. Such constraints can dilute your individuality and inadvertently signal messages about your capability or currency in the workplace that are misaligned with your actual attributes and contributions.

In crafting your professional identity, whether through clothes or alterations, the aim should not be to camouflage your age but to celebrate the individual you have become at every stage of your journey. Authenticity in how you present yourself—acknowledging that every wrinkle has been earned and every fresh perspective is valuable—can resonate more deeply than any attempt to conform to narrow age expectations.

Feeling the need to dress down or appear less successful to avoid intimidating or alienating prospects or clients is a notion that can inadvertently undermine your authority as a sales leader. Such a mentality stems from an attempt to foster relatability, but it risks projecting a lack of confidence in your abilities and devaluation of your professional expertise.

While approachability is admirable, compromising your professional identity can backfire. Prospects or clients may subconsciously interpret an overly casual appearance as a lack of investment in them or the engagement. It signals you aren't representing the premium value your solutions provide.

You want prospects or clients to feel respected and understood, not condescended to. A refined yet authentic presence inspires confidence that you grasp their needs as an advisor, not as a hierarchical sales professional. The key is finding the balance of projecting success without appearing unapproachable or out-of-touch.

Feeling pressure to match attire to the revenue level of accounts by dressing up or down based on the opportunity size is another self-imposed mindset that warrants re-examination. This pressure stems from wanting to over-align with perceived client expectations and socioeconomic backgrounds. And it can subtly communicate incomplete confidence in your role.

By strictly adhering to dressing "up" for larger accounts or "down" for smaller opportunities, you inadvertently create unspoken caste systems. It risks offending prospects or clients by assuming what their preferences are or what an "appropriate" sales professional should look like based solely on deal value.

As a leader, your priority is to embody the authority, expertise, and premium value your entire organization provides, regardless of individual deal economics. An authoritative yet relatable presence transcends opportunity tiers, allowing you to establish credibility through the merit of your insights and vision rather than arbitrary appearance cues.

Minimizing efforts under the assumption that sales skills, not appearance, is what matters is an understandable perspective for many sellers. The intention to prioritize substance over superficial style is admirable. But in leadership roles especially, putting minimal effort into your appearance can unintentionally signal complacency about your professional identity.

While certainly not the prime factor, your presence and intentional self-presentation directly impact how your leadership abilities are perceived, fair or not. Potential doubts can creep in about commitment and respect for the role when leaders appear disheveled or utterly indifferent about their imaging.

The reality is that top performance in sales leadership requires comprehensive and multifaceted efforts, including conscientious self-presentation. It's about projecting pride in yourself and the responsibilities of representing an organization with gravitas.

Limiting self-expression in professional settings is a self-limiting belief often rooted in deep-seated cultural, familial, and societal norms. You might find yourself trying hard to blend in, choosing muted colors, conservative cuts, and subdued accessories that won't rock the boat. This learned behavior, ingrained from an early age, can become a barrier to showcasing the full richness of your personality and professional potential.

But this inclination to blend in fails to recognize the power and importance of professional branding in today's business landscape. Authentic self-expression through clothing is a form of nonverbal communication that speaks volumes about your confidence, creativity, and leadership style. It's about striking a balance between respecting workplace decorum and embracing the distinctive qualities that set you apart.

By gently pushing against those inherited boundaries of self-expression, you open the door to a wardrobe that's not just acceptable but also memorable and true to who you are. The goal is not to disregard the influence of family, culture, or tradition but to evolve those influences into a personal style that complements your professional journey. It's about allowing yourself to shine within the framework of your professional environment, contributing your unique voice to the chorus in a way that is harmoniously yours.

Assuming the "perfection" burden is a self-imposed standard that leads you to believe every aspect of your appearance must be flawless. Rooted in the idea that respect and competence are tied to a faultless image, this perfection belief places immense pressure on you to maintain an impeccable facade at all times. This burden is not just about appearing professional. It's deeply intertwined with the fear of judgment and the desire for acceptance, leading to heightened anxiety and a critical self-view.

But the quest for perfection is unattainable and obscures the truth that authenticity and relatability are more compelling than flawlessness. The most respected leaders present themselves as human—approachable, genuine, and capable of embracing their imperfections.

Releasing yourself from the perfection burden doesn't mean abandoning self-care or professionalism. It means redefining what those concepts mean to you. It's about accepting minor imperfections and recognizing that your value as a sales leader is not solely contingent on an immaculate appearance. This shift in perspective can liberate you from over-scrutiny, reducing anxiety and fostering a more confident, authentic professional identity.

These are just a few of the self-limiting standards some of us might impose upon ourselves, shadow uniforms that can unconsciously shape our professional journey.

But it's crucial to always remember that your value in the workplace extends far beyond the confines of your look of leadership or the perfection of your presentation. Your expertise, your insights, and your contributions cannot be diminished by the superficial. Only in recognizing and challenging these self-imposed barriers can you grant yourself the freedom to express your professional identity more confidently.

Dressing Beyond the Code: Situational Awareness

In modern sales leadership, when the look of leadership can swing from boardroom formal to start-up casual, the concept of situational awareness is not just beneficial, it's imperative. Understanding the nuances of each context means you can navigate spaces with the acumen your role demands. It's about reading the room or the moment and adapting your appearance accordingly which, in turn, communicates your agility and attunement to the subtleties of the situation.

Situational awareness speaks to the ability to discern what is appropriate beyond written dress codes, industry norms, or even the personal standards you may set for yourself. It's recognizing there are occasions when the usual rules do not apply, and a different approach is called for, one that aligns with the unique dynamics of the current environment or event.

There will be times when the rigidity of formal clothes may be counterproductive, just as there will be moments when overly casual wear might undermine the gravity of your role. Situational awareness is the compass that guides you through these decisions, ensuring that your look contributes positively to the narrative of your sales leadership. It allows you to embody the versatility that is increasingly required of sales leaders today—not just in thought and action, but in the visual rhetoric of your professional identity. Hence, at times you'll need to . . .

Consider times of crisis or significant organizational change when sales leaders may forgo traditional business outfits for something that reflects both solidarity with their team and adaptability. In such scenarios it's less about form and more about symbolism and pragmatism. Think of company restructuring or mergers, a product recall, a critical sales project phase, a worldwide crisis, or a natural disaster. In such instances, choosing a look that is practical, durable, and less formal is crucial.

These choices, intentional and considerate, signal that you're fully engaged and empathetic to the challenges at hand. It's about rolling up your sleeves, both metaphorically and literally, to lead with empathy and readiness, emphasizing that sales leadership isn't just about directing from above but about being right there with your team.

Accept that practicality can beat professionalism or personal style. In the diverse environments that define our work, practical considerations often have to influence our look of leadership. As a speaker at a sales conference under the glaring focus of the stage lights, you're compelled to select clothes that won't clash with the technology around you. Your clothing should be amenable to the microphones, the lights, and the movement across the stage, just as your grooming should be a touch more polished to ensure your expressiveness translates across the room.

Similarly, if you are a sales leader in manufacturing, when you step out from your corporate office to visit a production site, you may need to adapt your attire, not just to ensure safety and practicality but to exemplify you understand the circumstances and environment your team members work in.

In these situations your look of leadership is not just about looking the part but about facilitating the part. Your look serves as a reminder that, sometimes, practicality must take precedence over professional polish or personal style. It's in these moments that your look becomes a tool of the trade that is integral to the performance of your professional duties.

Understand that you are a sales leader at all times, not just during business hours. This omnipresent leadership means that perception is continuous, and the silent dialogue of your look of leadership is always engaged. You need to remember you are a visible symbol of someone in a position of influence in your organization, industry, or personal identity 24/7/365.

Even in the absence of direct reports or colleagues, your look of leadership should always subtly communicate your role and readiness for engagement. This means at a coffee shop where a chance encounter with a potential client or partner could occur, your choice of outfit should bridge the gap between personal downtime and professional readiness. On the plane headed to your next sales conference, potential sponsors could be evaluating your appearance before you even have a chance to speak with them. While volunteering, whether for a cause related to your industry or something personal, your clothes still speak to your commitment to sales leadership and community. Even in the digital world your leadership is constantly on display. How you present yourself in video calls from home or in your profile picture on professional networking sites always should reflect the consistency of your professional identity.

In all those contexts and many more, embodying the essence of sales leadership in your presentation is key. It's about strategically selecting clothing that feels authentic to you while respecting the perception of leadership you've cultivated. This conscious curation of your out-of-office look is a testament to the perpetual nature of your professional identity.

As a leader, it's also your role to guide your team members in understanding this concept. Encourage them to consider their visual appearance as an extension of their professional identity, no matter the setting. Foster an understanding that there's always a level of consideration in how each team member reflects the shared identity of your organization.

Your leadership in this aspect sets the tone, signaling to your team that professional identity is a constant that is ingrained in the fabric of who you are as a professional collective. By guiding your team in these nuances, you reinforce the brand and reputation of your organization, strengthening public confidence in both individual sales leaders and the organization itself.

Embrace situational awareness as a key tool in your sales leadership arsenal, letting it guide you in making sartorial choices that resonate with each unique context. As you model this awareness, inspire your team to do the same, encouraging them to see their professional identity as a constant reflection of their dedication to your organization's shared mission.

By cultivating a culture of situational awareness that permeates every level of your organization, you'll create a team that understands and effectively wields the power of visual communication in every interaction.

Remember: your look of leadership is about the collective identity you represent as well as the values, expertise, and professionalism that define your organization and industry.

So as you navigate modern sales leadership, let situational awareness be your guide, helping you craft a look that is dynamic, authentic, adaptable, and impactful. Use it wisely and strategically to inspire others because, in the end, it's about living, breathing, and embodying the true essence of a sales leader who understands and harnesses the power of your presence for the greater good.

Chapter 6
Leaders Look Respectful

Failing to Respect Yourself
Casts Doubt on Your Ability to
Respect Others.

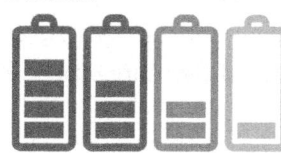

Chapter 6:
Leaders Look Respectful

The concept of respect is foundational in any sphere, and in sales leadership roles it's a cornerstone that cannot be overstressed. It's the glue that not only binds the strands of integrity, credibility, and authority in a leader's tapestry, it bridges the gap between traditional expectations and modern leadership paradigms. Respect is a multifaceted gem that particularly reflects sales leaders' regard for themselves, their positions, their teams, and the collective ethos of the organizations they steer. At its core, respect demands an unwavering commitment to professional excellence that pushes beyond basic competence to embody the aspirational ideal of unimpeachable character, uncompromising expertise, and inspirational influence. For those empowered to lead sales teams, this pursuit of respected stature must permeate every aspect of their presence and actions.

For sales leaders, dressing with respect is a nuanced dance between expressing individuality and honoring the mantle of their roles. It articulates values and sets a tone for interactions, speaking volumes before a word is even uttered. When meeting with prospects or clients, a sales leader's respectful presence conveys an unspoken commitment to conducting business at the highest professional standards. It instills confidence that serious matters will be handled with gravitas and deserving discernment, not frivolous showmanship.

A respected leader's look serves as a silent ambassador, representing their organization's brand ethos while simultaneously personifying the individual leader's own distinctive expertise and background to establish immediate authority. The styling cues of a respected presence harmonize the organizational identity with the personal, enabling those interactions to transcend traditionally transactional "selling" to become trusted advisory consultations from opening introductions.

When sales leaders choose a look of leadership that resonates with respect, they make a statement about their personal standards and their dedication to their roles. It's a visible manifestation of self-regard and a sophisticated acknowledgment of the tremendous responsibility they carry as vision-owners for their prospects' or clients' success and their team's performance potential. An intentional wardrobe sends a clarion signal to others that the sales leader respects the enormous influence and stewardship duties inherent in their position.

But the flip side—a lack of respect displayed through self-presentation choices—can undermine a sales leader's authority. Lack of respect perpetuates outdated stereotypes that undermine the legitimacy of the modern sales profession as an elite discipline of business strategy and relationship nurturing. It erodes hard-earned trust with prospects or clients and partners who entrust their biggest ambitions to the expertise being represented.

And, ultimately, even the most temporary lapse into disrespectful self-presentation can lead to an organizational atmosphere that negatively impacts team engagement, retention of top talent, and the overall cultural fabric. Such seemingly minor missteps in upholding a respected presence can directly lead to diminished team morale, reduced ability to secure new business as first impressions falter, and lost credibility as an authoritative voice in the high-stakes negotiations that decide companies' fates.

Respect is not a one-way street. As a sales leader, when you broadcast respect for yourself through your look of leadership, you establish the uncompromising benchmark for those you lead. In doing so, you are infinitely more likely to garner that same deference and professional esteem in return. This cycle of mutual respect becomes the transformative catalyst for cultivating an organizational environment where accountability, ethos, and excellence can collectively flourish across teams, partnerships, and client relationships.

This mutual acknowledgment of respected presence as a non-negotiable standard is essential for forging the strong, productive relationships that generate consistent, high-performing, empowered teams unified by bonds of trust. By personifying the ideal of respected leadership through your intentional imaging choices, you organically establish the invaluable workplace dynamic that supports both individual and collective aspirations for ethical success through unwavering mutual investment.

Your respectful look of leadership is a visual testament to your personal and organizational dedication to elevating the sales profession itself. Whether in the corporate boardroom formulating enterprise-level strategy, in the field executing complex solutions for prospects' or clients' biggest ambitions, making the opening pitch to secure landscape-shifting deals, or simply walking the sales floor as an inspirational standard-bearer, your respectful presence reinforces an atmosphere of integrity and demonstrates the sanctity of how business gets done. Conversely, even unintentional deviations from upholding that respected stature can foment atmospheres of cynicism and ethical apathy that can undermine the purpose and value propositions you've been entrusted to deliver.

Your look of respectful leadership can acknowledge the trust placed in you by upper managers, prospects, clients, and stakeholders who have deemed you worthy of impacting their most precious assets and long-term growth trajectories.

It can communicate your studious consideration about cultural, organizational and social norms informing the contexts in which you engage. It illustrates that, for you, a respectful look of leadership is not merely about fleeting fabrics, trends, or fashion-chasing. Rather, it's an intentionally crafted conduit of authority and communication for your teams', prospects', and clients' most pivotal moments and transformational decision-making.

It's a Sign of Self-Respect

In the intricate dance of leadership, self-respect is the foundational rhythm. It is the silent force that shapes your actions and decisions, influencing how you are perceived and how effectively you can inspire others. Self-respect is not merely a personal attribute; it is a professional necessity that underscores your worth and fortifies your presence. It is the starting point from which all other aspects of leadership emanate, providing a solid base upon which to build credibility, trust, and influence. Without self-respect, the façade of leadership crumbles, revealing a hollow core that cannot sustain the weight of responsibility and authority. Self-respect is the seed from which the fruits of effective leadership grow, and nurturing it is crucial to achieving enduring success.

Self-respect is not about displaying self-importance but acknowledging your inherent worth. It manifests in the meticulous care you take in yourself, reflecting an inner ethos of precision and attention to detail that's paramount for sales leadership success. It's the veteran global VP of enterprise sales whose impeccable power suits radiate self-respect that demands others to lean in when they speak about their biggest operational challenges and strategic visions. It's the director of business development at an elite boutique winery whose refined wear personifies their personal investment in that respected heritage brand and the once-in-a-lifetime tasting experiences they facilitate for the world's most discerning collectors.

It's the medical device sales leader so attuned to self-presentation that hospital administrators immediately experience their presence as that of a respected fellow professional whose goal is to improve patient care, not just move units from a vendor. Their self-respect radiates through the thoughtful quality of material selections; the cohesive sophistication of their styling transcends the latest fads; and their prioritization of impeccable tailoring and grooming habits exude palpable expertise. Even the most subtle accessories and accents broadcast their individualized personal identities of respected leadership and credible authority.

Self-respect is a visual representation of your professional ethos. Dressing with self-respect is not merely about the price tag, designer label cachet, or ostentatious displays of unwarranted wealth. So let's be pragmatic: thoughtful financial investment into building a respected leadership wardrobe is undeniably an act of self-valuation. It's a make-or-break commitment to the undisputed mindset that representing yourself, your team, and your organizational priorities at the highest level is worthy of purposeful resource allocation, not simply an indulgent afterthought. Just as critical as funding, it's about selecting garments and styling choices that emphasize your strengths while elevating perceived professional stature. It's suit cuts that flatter your natural silhouette. It's accessories and grooming touches that amplify your most compelling personal features and broadcast your distinctive flair. It's curating an aesthetic experience—one as thorough and coherent as the sales narratives you've mastered—that breathes new life into the archetype of respected leadership itself.

Self-respect requires financial investment but not superfluous extravagance. At its core, cultivating a respected professional identity is about ensuring that every detailed component is curated with equal zeal, precision, and philosophical conviction as the complex solutions, services, and overarching vision you champion daily.

Everything must integrate as seamless chapters within the greater story you seek to inspire, underscoring your unwavering self-respect as a steadfast guide worthy of being followed. This commitment to embodying a respected presence must persist as a constant across all professional and personal contexts, not simply make cursory appearances between office hours. This "armor" of self-respect isn't rooted in vapid vanity. Rather, it's the outward personification of the pride, diligence, and resolute self-actualization you've earned through years of committed excellence within the sales arena's most elite battlegrounds.

Self-respect requires relentless dedication but not superfluous extravagance. It's about shrewd resource allocation to secure the components that empower you to look and feel like the respected tour de force your office deserves. This effort involves carefully curating your wardrobe, grooming habits, and overall presentation to ensure that every detail reflects your commitment to excellence. Investing in high-quality, well-fitting clothing and accessories that complement your professional identity is a testament to your self-respect and your understanding of the importance of visual impact in leadership. Moreover, self-respect extends beyond material investments to include the time and effort dedicated to maintaining your appearance. This means regular grooming routines, staying updated on fashion trends that align with your professional identity, and consistently presenting yourself in a manner that exudes confidence and authority. By doing so, you not only enhance your own presence but set a standard for those around you.

You can never credibly inspire teams, prospects, clients, or stakeholders to elevate their own standards if you haven't continually invested in elevating yours as their aspirational exemplar through the physical manifestations of your persona. Your dedication to self-respect serves as a powerful example that encourages others to prioritize their professional appearance and personal development.

Your example creates a culture of excellence within your organization where high standards are the norm and every individual is motivated to present their best self.

The relentless dedication to self-respect in your appearance is not just about looking good, it's about embodying the principles of leadership, discipline, and self-worth. It's a visual affirmation of your readiness to lead, inspire, and achieve at the highest levels. This commitment to self-respect ensures that you are always prepared to face challenges with poise and confidence, reinforcing your position as a leader who commands respect and admiration.

Self-respect involves consistency. Consistency in your appearance, whether during formal meetings or in casual settings, showcases your reliability and steadfastness. It signals that you are dependable and unwavering in your values and professional standards. Consider the sales leader who maintains a professional appearance, not just for high-stakes client presentations but also during casual internal meetings or while working remotely. This unwavering commitment to a consistent, professional appearance demonstrates an inherent self-respect as well as a respect for the professional environment, regardless of the occasion. It sends a clear message to colleagues, prospects, clients, and stakeholders that you are always prepared, always professional, and always committed to excellence. For instance, think of the senior sales executive who, even during virtual meetings, ensures their attire, background, and overall presentation remain impeccable. This level of consistency reinforces their image as a reliable and dedicated leader who takes every interaction seriously, whether face-to-face or screen-to-screen.

Furthermore, this consistency in appearance translates into consistency in performance. When a leader takes pride in their presentation, it often reflects a meticulous approach to their work and interactions. It showcases their attention to detail and their commitment to maintaining high standards in every aspect of their professional life.

This reliability builds trust and respect among peers, prospects, and clients, reinforcing their professional identity. By presenting yourself consistently, you create a stable and predictable image that others can rely on. It eliminates any doubts about your professionalism and dedication, making it clear that you uphold your values and standards unwaveringly. This steadfastness not only enhances your credibility but inspires confidence in those who work with you and for you.

Self-respect includes taking care of your physical and mental health. A healthy body reflects discipline and self-care, both crucial aspects of self-respect that directly contribute to your professional identity and look of leadership. Your physical well-being is not just about aesthetics but about the vitality and energy you bring into every interaction. Maintaining a vibrant and energetic presence enhances your leadership by showcasing your ability to manage and prioritize your health amidst professional demands.

But mental health is equally significant. A calm and composed conduct reflects inner strength and stability, essential traits for any leader. Prioritizing mental clarity ensures that you can navigate challenges with a level head and make decisions with confidence. This holistic approach to well-being underscores your commitment to excellence in every aspect of your professional life. By exuding physical health and mental clarity, you project an image of resilience and reliability that forms a critical part of your professional identity. It translates into a commanding presence, making you a more effective and inspiring leader. This dedication to maintaining your well-being not only benefits you personally, it also sets a powerful example for your team, reinforcing the importance of self-care as a cornerstone of professional success.

In sales leadership, your look is not solely defined by your wardrobe but also by the overall presence you bring into the room. A well-maintained physique and mental sharpness complement your attire, ensuring that every aspect of your appearance exudes competence and credibility. identity as a leader worthy of respect and admiration.

As you navigate the landscape of leadership, remember that self-respect is not a static trait but a dynamic force that continually shapes your journey. It is the quiet confidence that allows you to face challenges head-on, the unwavering belief in your capabilities that drives you to strive for excellence, and the internal compass that guides your ethical standards.

Embracing self-respect transforms not only how others see you but how you see yourself, fostering a sense of purpose and fulfillment that transcends external validations. It is a reminder that true leadership begins within, and by cultivating self-respect you unlock the potential to lead with authenticity, inspire with integrity, and achieve with unwavering resolve.

In the end, the greatest testament to your leadership will not be the accolades you receive but the respect you earn, starting with the respect you give yourself.

It Shows You Respect Others

As a sales leader your look of leadership is not merely a matter of personal style or preference; it is a powerful communication tool that conveys your respect for those around you. In a world where first impressions are often formed in an instant, the way you present yourself can significantly impact how others perceive your intentions, professionalism, and values.

Your appearance speaks volumes about your regard for the diverse individuals and communities you engage daily. It demonstrates that you value their perspectives, honor their contributions, and are committed to fostering an environment of mutual respect and understanding. By embodying respect in your appearance, you set the tone for a culture in which everyone feels valued and empowered, ultimately leading to stronger relationships and greater success.

Your look of leadership impacts how your family and friends are perceived. The way you present yourself extends beyond your professional sphere and impacts how those closest to you are perceived. When you maintain a respectful appearance, you honor the trust and support of those who have been part of your journey. This broader respect reinforces the trust and admiration others have for your family and network, elevating the collective reputation of all connected to you. Your appearance serves as a testament to the values you share with your inner circle, showcasing a commitment to integrity and excellence that uplifts everyone associated with you. It demonstrates that you are mindful of the impression you make, not just for yourself but for the broader circle you influence.

Your look of leadership is a signal of respect to your team members. As a sales leader, the way you present yourself sets the tone for the entire team. Your commitment to maintaining a respectful appearance signals to your team that you value their contributions and are dedicated to leading by example. This respect fosters a culture of mutual trust and high standards, encouraging team members to mirror you. By showing that you hold yourself to high standards, you set a powerful example, motivating your team to also strive for excellence.

Your look of leadership reflects the values of your organization. Every interaction you have, whether internal or external, reflects on the organization you represent. This commitment to upholding the organization's standards enhances its reputation and strengthens its position in the industry. Your appearance serves as a constant reminder of the organization's dedication to excellence and ethical conduct. Your respect for the organization is evident in how you communicate its values and uphold its brand visually, ensuring that your personal identity aligns seamlessly with the corporate identity.

Your look of leadership reflects on those who lead you. As a sales leader your respectful appearance is not only a reflection of your personal standards but of those who lead and mentor you. Your look of leadership sends a powerful message about the values and expectations of upper management, the senior leaders and executives you represent. By maintaining a respectful appearance, you honor the trust and responsibility bestowed upon you.

Your respectful appearance is a testament to your respect for your industry. As a representative of your profession, your appearance should reflect the highest standards of your industry. This respect for your field demonstrates your commitment to its principles and your role in advancing its goals. By upholding those standards, you contribute to the overall credibility and prestige of your profession, setting a benchmark for others to follow.

Your look of leadership signals respect and reliability to your prospects and clients. A respectful appearance shows that you value their time and business, fostering trust and building stronger relationships. This respect is not just about looking professional but about demonstrating that you understand and appreciate the importance of the client's needs and priorities. This approach not only enhances client satisfaction but also sets the foundation for long-term partnerships built on mutual respect, showing prospects and clients that you value their business and are committed to providing exceptional service.

Your look of leadership should reflect respect for all stakeholders. Beyond the immediate circles of family, team members, prospects, and clients, a sales leader's respect must extend to all stakeholders, including partners, suppliers, and the broader community. This holistic respect ensures that every decision and action is guided by a commitment to ethical principles and long-term sustainability. It reflects a broader understanding of the interconnectedness of business and society and underscores your role as a responsible and visionary leader.

Your look of leadership should honor cultural diversity. The business landscape is a tapestry of diverse cultures and traditions. As a sales leader, showing respect for cultural differences in your appearance and interactions demonstrates your commitment to inclusivity. This respect builds bridges and fosters a more harmonious and productive business environment. By acknowledging and celebrating cultural diversity, you create an atmosphere in which all team members, prospects, and clients feel valued and respected. This respect is reflected in your willingness to learn about and adapt to different cultural norms and practices, enhancing your ability to connect with and inspire individuals from various backgrounds. This does not mean you have to dress differently based on every culture you encounter; rather, it means your look of leadership will not add friction points and, instead, will respect the diverse backgrounds of those you interact with.

Your look of leadership should respect religious diversity. Recognizing and honoring the diverse religious beliefs and values of your colleagues, prospects, clients, and partners is crucial in today's interconnected world. By showing respect for these differences through your appearance, you promote a culture of acceptance and mutual respect, which ensures that everyone feels valued, regardless of their religious or ethical background. This sensitivity fosters an inclusive workplace where individuals feel free to express their beliefs and values without fear of discrimination. Your professional appearance should avoid elements that could be perceived as disrespectful to various religious practices and, instead, show openness and respect in all your interactions.

Your look of leadership should respect generational diversity. The modern workplace is a blend of multiple generations, each bringing distinct perspectives and strengths. Respecting these generational differences in your presentation and interactions shows your appreciation for the diverse experiences and insights each generation offers.

By presenting yourself in a way that bridges generational gaps, you foster an inclusive environment. This approach enhances collaboration and innovation by leveraging the strengths and perspectives of each age group. Your look of leadership should demonstrate a respect for all generations, ensuring that you are approachable and relatable to everyone, regardless of age.

Your look of leadership should embrace gender diversity. As societal understanding of gender evolves, it's important to respect and acknowledge diverse gender identities. This respect not only supports those who identify outside traditional gender norms but also sets a precedent for acceptance and equality in the workplace. It reinforces your commitment to creating a space where everyone can thrive, free from discrimination or bias. By presenting yourself in a way that acknowledges and respects diverse gender identities, you foster an inclusive environment where everyone feels valued and respected. Ensure that your look of leadership avoids reinforcing outdated gender norms and, instead, promotes a culture of inclusivity and respect.

The way you present yourself as a sales leader is a profound act of respect that goes beyond superficial appearances. It is an affirmation of your commitment to the values and principles that underpin your professional and personal interactions. By consciously cultivating a look of leadership that honors the diverse identities and backgrounds of those you engage with, you create a powerful ripple effect that fosters inclusivity, trust, and collaboration. This dedication to respectful self-presentation not only enhances your credibility and influence but serves as a beacon of inspiration for others to follow. As you navigate the complexities of modern leadership, let your appearance be a testament to your unwavering respect for the humanity and dignity of every individual you encounter. This approach not only will elevate your own leadership journey but will contribute to building a more compassionate and connected professional world.

It's Not Always Reciprocated

Respect is an invaluable cornerstone of professional interactions, yet it is a stark reality that it's not always reciprocated. It might be your client who shows up disheveled at your meeting, your own upper management that doesn't represent the organization in the way it should, or a colleague whose lack of professionalism undermines the team's efforts.

As a sales leader who meticulously cultivates a respectful appearance, it can be disheartening to encounter individuals who do not extend the same courtesy. Despite your unwavering commitment to maintaining a respectful presence, inevitably there will be instances when others fail to mirror your values.

Understanding why this happens and how to navigate these challenges without compromising your own standards is essential for sustaining your integrity and leadership. There are numerous reasons others may not reciprocate the respect you consistently demonstrate, including the following:

- **Lack of awareness:** Some professionals may simply be unaware of the importance of maintaining a respectful appearance in professional settings. They might not recognize how their visual appearance affects others or understand the impact of a respectful look of leadership. This lack of awareness can lead to unintentional disrespect that stems from ignorance rather than malice. It's essential to understand that these individuals might not be acting out of ill will but from a place of unfamiliarity with professional standards.

- **Different standards:** Unfortunately, not everyone adheres to the same standards of visual appearance. Some professionals may prioritize their own interests above mutual respect, displaying a lack of consideration in their appearance that is self-serving or inconsiderate. Such actions undermine the collective effort and can create an atmosphere of resentment. As a leader, it is crucial to set and uphold high standards in your look of leadership, reinforcing the importance of a respectful and professional appearance in achieving shared goals.

- **Personal context:** You never know the full story. It's important to remember that everyone has a unique story and context that may not be immediately known. Personal struggles, health issues, cultural differences, or challenging circumstances can influence how people present themselves. You must be careful not to jump to conclusions or make assumptions about someone's lack of respect based solely on their appearance. Instead, approach such situations with empathy and understanding, recognizing that there may be unseen factors at play.

- **External pressures:** External pressures, such as tight deadlines, emergencies, or high-stress situations, can impact how professionals present themselves. These pressures might lead to moments when maintaining a respectful appearance is not a priority. You need to show understanding for these lapses and recognize they may only be temporary.

- **Personal insecurities:** Professionals who are insecure about their own appearance may exhibit disrespectful actions as a defensive mechanism. They might feel threatened by your look of leadership, causing them to undermine or dismiss your efforts in an attempt to bolster their own self-esteem. Understanding that such behavior often stems from a place of insecurity allows you to address it with empathy rather than frustration.

- **Economic constraints:** Not everyone has the same financial resources to invest in a professional wardrobe. Economic constraints can affect how professionals present themselves, leading to differences in appearance that might be mistaken for a lack of respect. While their financial limitations may be difficult for you, as a leader, to improve, it's important to create an understanding that a respectful visual appearance doesn't mean you have to break the bank.

- **Environmental influences:** Professionals might adopt a more casual or disheveled appearance because they see such appearances being modeled by others. This can create a vicious cycle in which a lack of attention to visual appearance becomes normalized, eroding respect. As a leader, it is vital that you recognize the impact of the organizational culture on the look of leadership and work proactively to cultivate a more respectful environment. This includes setting clear expectations for appearance, modeling a respectful look of leadership, and addressing issues of neglect promptly and effectively.

- **Rebellion against norms:** Like it or not, some professionals might intentionally reject conventional standards of respectful appearance as a form of personal expression or rebellion against what they perceive as outdated norms. Such behavior can be a conscious choice to challenge the status quo and advocate for a more relaxed, inclusive definition of professionalism. There's not much you can do other than respect their choice and maintain your own standards. If they are in your sphere of influence, you can continue to mentor them or, unfortunately, you may have to consider if they are the right person for your team.

In a world where respect is not always reciprocated, maintaining your own standards of respect is an act of resilience and integrity. It is a testament to your character and commitment to leadership excellence. This steadfast adherence to your values, even in the face of non-reciprocity, sets you apart as a true leader. After all, respect is a reflection of your inner ethos. It's a gift to yourself and those you lead, regardless of whether it is reciprocated.

Chapter 7
Leaders Look Controlled

The More You Control,
the Better the Outcome.

Chapter 7:
Leaders Look Controlled

The ability to strategize and innovate is an essential part of sales leadership, and it profoundly influences sales leaders' professional identity. The tapestry of how they are perceived is intricate, demanding each piece be positioned with intention. This art of self-presentation in which every choice, from clothing to communication style, is deliberate constructs a sales leader's comprehensive professional identity in the eyes of the world.

Envision your professional identity as a continual curation of your professional persona. Every detail, from the subtlety of your accessories to the precision of your clothing, is a declaration of the control you possess over your personal and professional narrative. It's a powerful statement that says, "I am the author of my fate; I steer the course of my success," and it speaks volumes about your self-assurance and the respect you command, silently yet resoundingly.

You, as a sales leader guiding others, take the reins of your professional identity, not by chance, but through a disciplined routine that echoes your professional diligence. You realize that although not every perception can be influenced, neglecting to consciously craft your professional identity would be to allow others to fill in the blanks, often with inaccurate information. Thus, intentionally shaping your narrative ensures that it remains firmly in your hands and is an accurate reflection of your ability to guide not only your own path but the trajectory of those who follow your lead.

Taking control of your professional identity is not an act of vanity but a strategic move. It's an affirmation that, even though you can't control every perception, you can lay a solid, indelible foundation that resonates with the identity you aim to project.

Why leave such a powerful aspect to serendipity? Why permit happenstance to dictate what can be shaped with purpose and precision?

Sales leaders who leave indelible marks are those who wield their professional identity as a vibrant and influential facet of their leadership repertoire. They choose their wardrobe, they mind their grooming, and they conduct themselves not solely for style but for the substantive legacy they're building. They are the ones who seize the narrative, orchestrating not only their strategic boardroom presence but the unspoken stories evoked by their conduct.

Like a skilled CEO who strategizes and executes each business move with precision and foresight, as a sales leader you must embrace every tool at your disposal. Your career is a tapestry of roles and achievements, yes, but also of your conscious effort to sculpt your professional identity. This process features the following factors:

- **Self-awareness,** where reflection becomes as routine as strategy meetings.

- **Self-care,** where discipline in personal presentation is akin to financial stewardship.

- **Self-promotion,** where advocating for your achievements is as crucial as marketing your organization's successes.

In cultivating your professional identity with such intention and consideration, you do more than advance your career trajectory, you lay down a pathway for excellence.

Self-Awareness and Self-Reflection

Self-awareness and self-reflection are pillars of professional growth and leadership, crucial for sales leaders who are forging their paths in various industries. This introspective journey starts with a deep dive into your strengths, vulnerabilities, and core values as well as an honest assessment of the effect you have on others in the workplace and the broader business environment or community. This process is about continuous inward exploration, challenging yourself with difficult questions about motives, unconscious biases, and the ripple effects of your decisions. It means pausing after each significant event to evaluate successes and missteps, fostering a culture of perpetual learning and personal and professional development. Such reflection is indispensable in the dynamic, high-stakes scenarios that sales leaders frequently navigate, offering a means to evolve from every experience.

Beyond personal reflection, self-awareness for sales leaders means understanding how their professional identity influences their organization's culture. It's about recognizing the pivotal role they play within their teams, how their leadership style affects team cohesion, and how their strategic decisions drive the organization's progress and success. This self-awareness should profoundly shape your look of leadership, guiding you to cultivate a visual appearance that is congruent with your role and the expectations of those who look to you for guidance. Contemplating your look of leadership is far from superficial; it is a strategic consideration of how your appearance can affirm or undermine perceptions of your competence and professionalism.

This includes considering the messages sent by certain styles, colors, fabrics, patterns, and levels of formality. It involves asking yourself questions such as, "Does my attire convey the authority and expertise expected of my role?" or "Is my appearance accessible and reassuring to individuals from diverse backgrounds?" or "How does my personal style affect my team's perception of my leadership?"

As a sales leader, the way you present yourself should answer those questions and mirror your core principles. It's about deciding to wear clothing that doesn't just fit the body but fits the moment and the mission. Your look of leadership should communicate that you're grounded in expertise, yet your feet walk the same ground as those you're leading. It's how your professionalism doesn't overshadow your humanity but accentuates it.

Self-Care and Self-Discipline

Self-care and self-discipline stand as crucial supports for both personal well-being and professional prowess. For sales leaders, self-care often takes on an added layer of significance. It's about nurturing your physical, emotional, and mental health, which is especially important given the tendency for sales leaders to prioritize the care of others at the expense of their own well-being.

It's no secret that the ingrained focus on caretaking can make it difficult for sales leaders to turn the lens of care inward. Yet, just as the familiar airline safety instruction advises us to secure our own oxygen masks before assisting others, your self-care operates on the same principle: if you neglect your own well-being, it will manifest in your ability to lead. To be seen as capable of nurturing and guiding others, you must visibly take care of yourself first.

This isn't about self-indulgence but about fundamental maintenance that enables effective leadership. It's a clear signal to your team and colleagues that you are well-prepared to manage the multifaceted demands of leadership. It communicates that you understand the importance of balance and are equipped to handle the various responsibilities and individuals who rely on your guidance and expertise.

Discipline is the commitment to maintaining these self-care practices regularly and making choices that align with your long-term goals and values, even when they require sacrifice or delay of gratification.

This includes a broad spectrum of habits that keep you at your best, be it through adequate sleep, nutritious eating, physical activity, or mindfulness practices. These activities are not luxuries but necessities that enable you to perform at your peak.

Discipline, especially in the context of self-care, also involves setting boundaries to protect your time and energy. It means being able to say no to nonessential demands and recognizing when you need to step back and recharge. It not only prevents burnout but models healthy behavior for your team members, reinforcing the importance of well-being in sustaining high performance.

But the irony lies in the fact that although discipline may not be a struggle in its application to external tasks, there is a nuanced challenge in turning that discipline inward. It's a nuanced imbalance where the rigor applied to caring for others isn't always matched by the discipline needed for self-nourishment and rejuvenation. Acknowledging and addressing this imbalance is crucial, for disciplined self-care is the reservoir from which the strength to lead others is drawn. Only when leaders apply the same level of discipline to their own well-being as they do to their professional duties can they embody the comprehensive excellence that leadership demands.

This conduct doesn't require perfection or a stringent adherence to unrealistic standards of professional identity. Rather, it requires a presence that reflects the seriousness with which you approach your responsibilities and the trust placed in you.

Self-Improvement and Self-Promotion

In sales leadership, continuous personal and professional development and strategic self-promotion underscore the ever-evolving journey of personal and professional growth. As the CEO of your own career, embracing personal and professional development means recognizing that the pursuit of excellence never ends. It is a commitment to ongoing education, skill refinement, and personal evolution.

At the same time, self-promotion, which is often misunderstood and can carry a stigma of self-aggrandizement, is a vital component of leadership. It's about articulating and celebrating your achievements, not out of vanity but as a powerful form of advocacy for the value you bring to your organization. It involves illuminating your contributions in a manner that fosters recognition and serves as a beacon for others. This approach not only paves the way for your own advancement but also raises the profile of your team's efforts, aligning with and advancing the collective objectives of your organization and industry.

Self-promotion for many sales leaders can be an intricate challenge, partly rooted in societal expectations and norms. Historically, sales leaders have been encouraged to be collaborative and communal rather than assertive and self-promoting, leading to an internal conflict for many of us when it comes time to highlight our own accomplishments.

Many sales leaders grapple with the fine line between being perceived as confident and being labeled as self-important. They often worry that by asserting their achievements, they may encounter backlash or be accused of not being team-oriented. This concern is compounded by the imposter syndrome that many high-achieving sales leaders experience when, despite their accomplishments, they fear being exposed as a fraud.

There's also a cultural component to consider. In some cultures, speaking highly of yourself is seen as boasting, which can be socially frowned upon. This cultural belief can influence sales leaders' willingness to engage in self-promotion, especially in multicultural workplaces.

Despite the obstacles, self-promotion is a critical skill for career advancement. It requires a balanced approach that aligns with your values, leverages the right platforms, and focuses on sharing successes in a way that celebrates the team's effort. The goal is to normalize self-promotion as a healthy part of professional life, shifting the narrative to one in which sales leaders can proudly and rightfully claim their achievements without hesitation.

Self-improvement for some sales leaders translates into a relentless pursuit of perfection. There's an ingrained belief that to succeed you must not only match but exceed the standards set by predecessors or counterparts, every single time. This drive, although admirable, can morph into an endless quest where "good enough" rarely is, and the goal posts of achievement keep moving.

This pressure to continuously enhance skills and knowledge while striving for flawlessness can create an exhausting cycle of self-imposed expectations.

For sales leaders, the journey of personal and professional development should be reframed from a race toward an unattainable ideal of perfection to a journey of growth that values progress over perfection. It should be about recognizing the merit in each step of your personal and professional development, celebrating your small victories, and understanding that making mistakes is a natural part of your learning process. It should be about recognizing that true personal and professional development isn't about reaching a pinnacle of perfection but about continuously growing, learning, and contributing in meaningful ways without the overshadowing pressure to be flawless.

As you navigate the landscapes of leadership, remember this: your approach to these topics directly influences your look of leadership. Your appearance isn't merely about the clothes you wear. Instead, your look of leadership embodies the confidence with which you share your accomplishments and the grace with which you pursue personal and professional development. Your look of leadership incorporates the assured way you carry yourself, knowing you've earned your place at the table. It reflects the mindful choices you make that demonstrate not a pursuit of perfection but a commitment to continuous improvement. It shows the care you put into yourself and the awareness that you deserve it.

Your look of leadership is a visible extension of where you stand on your journey. Let it be an armor of empowerment, woven with threads of your personal narrative of success and resilience.

This look of leadership—your look—isn't static. It evolves as you do, shaped by every choice that positions you as an expert in your field and by every step of personal and professional development that keeps you dynamic and forward-thinking. It's a look that respects where you've been and anticipates where you'll go, all while asserting the undeniable impact you make every single day.

Be Prepared for the Predictable and the Unpredictable

In a world teeming with much uncertainty, the preparedness to face both the predictable and the unpredictable becomes a defining trait of effective leadership. As you stand at the nexus of daily shifts, the ability to anticipate and adapt is essential. Hence, your look of leadership should be curated not just for aesthetic appeal but for its strategic function. Curating it with intention is an exercise in scenario planning, a rehearsal for the diverse roles you must play to align the tangible elements of your look with the intangible dynamics of your day. Embarking on this sartorial strategy requires contemplation, a series of reflective questions that may guide your choices and ensure your look of leadership is congruent with your professional objectives, for example:

- What's the big picture for today?
- What's the occasion?
- With whom will you be interacting?
- What will they be wearing?
- What will your client be wearing?
- What will your upper management be wearing?
- What will your colleagues be wearing?
- What will your team members be wearing?
- Where are you going to meet?
- Where may you be heading after you meet?
- How will you get there?
- Who else could you randomly meet today?
- What message do you have to deliver today?

Although those questions are universally relevant to professionals across the board, as a sales leader there are additional layers to consider, so here are some additional questions you might ask yourself:

- What types of sales scenarios will I be facing today (e.g. initial prospecting calls, product demos, contract negotiations, closing meetings)?
- Will I be delivering formal presentations or participating in casual conversations?
- Will I be transitioning between internal team updates and external client meetings seamlessly?
- Are there any cultural considerations or social norms to account for with certain prospects or clients?
- How might my schedule or travel impact my ability to refresh my appearance throughout the day?
- Could I be recorded on video or photographed for company/marketing materials?
- How does my attire empower me in spaces where sales leaders are underrepresented?
- Does my outfit align with my leadership style while challenging traditional sales norms?
- How does my attire today honor my personal identity and the narrative I wish to convey as a sales leader?
- How does this attire serve as a model for other sales professionals in my organization who are striving to define their own professional identity?
- In what ways can I use my attire to make a statement about the inclusivity and diversity I champion as a leader?
- Can my attire choices today inspire confidence in other sales professionals looking to break glass ceilings within the industry?
- How might my clothing choices today mitigate bias or change perceptions about sales leaders' roles in leadership?

The answers to those questions form the cornerstone of your professional identity. They guide you to select a look of leadership that not only matches the situations you'll face but also allow you to shine in your leadership role, demonstrating intention and preparedness. By strategically planning, you're taking command of an element of your career that's too often left to happenstance. This proactive approach is a vital step in crafting an image of leadership that says you are just as formidable in your appearance as you are in your professional skill set. It's an intentional choice, the armor of a leader poised to tackle the day's challenges.

It's Not Only about Clothes

Yes, looking the part is important, but it's merely the opening act. It's true that a professional appearance can open doors and instill confidence, but it's the substance behind the style that defines a leader. Remember: it's not only about the clothes you wear, it also revolves around embodying the values and responsibilities of your role through every aspect of your professional identity.

Your visual appearance might introduce you, but your behavior tells the story of who you truly are. Your communication underscores your competence and empathy, your digital footprint extends your influence beyond the physical walls of any organization, and your environment reflects your professional standards.

BEHAVIOR: Across the dynamic arenas of various organizations your behavior carries as much weight as your appearance does, if not more. The way you conduct yourself—your actions, reactions, and interactions—becomes a living testament to your leadership and professionalism. Consider this: you may dress impeccably with every detail curated to convey authority, but if your behavior does not align with your presentation, your appearance becomes an empty shell. In the daily demands of sales leadership where challenges and opportunities often coincide, your behavior is a guiding light for your team members. It should embody the virtues your look of leadership suggests.

Your behavior also extends to how you handle the unexpected. In any industry, crises are not a matter of if but when. You might find yourself navigating a critical sales negotiation in which your leadership is crucial. Here, your composed conduct amidst adversity, your clear directives, and your swift decision-making reflect the respect and control suggested by your professional appearance. You must be the steady presence in times of tumult, the clarity in times of uncertainty, and the empathy in every strategic decision you make. Let your behavior be the complement to your look of leadership, not a contradiction, and vice versa.

As a leader in sales your behavior not only shapes your position within your organization but also profoundly influences your relationships with prospects or clients and their decision-making processes throughout the sales cycle. Leadership, in this case, transcends mere transactional interactions to embody trust, integrity, and reliability, qualities that must resonate consistently through your actions because they set a critical precedent.

Acting with confidence and transparency, you nurture an environment of trust and openness. This behavior influences not just how your team perceives you but how willingly they follow your lead and embrace open communication and collaboration. The tone you set through your behavior impacts everything from team morale to performance standards.

In addition, your behavior significantly shapes how prospects or clients perceive and interact with your organization. Prospects or clients invest in relationships, not just products or services. Demonstrating ethical behavior and a consistent, reliable presence builds a foundational trust that is crucial during negotiations and pivotal in decision-making processes. How you handle challenges reassures prospects or clients of your capability to manage crises, bolstering their confidence in your leadership.

Each phase of the sales cycle offers unique opportunities to exhibit leadership behaviors that go beyond mere communication. Here are some examples:

- **Prospecting and initial contact:** The professionalism and respect you show during these early interactions set the stage for the relationship.

- **Needs assessment:** Demonstrating attention to detail and a genuine interest in understanding the client's needs can build substantial rapport without a word said about solutions.

- **Presentation and proposal:** Your ability to present yourself and your proposals with confidence—without overtly selling—speaks volumes about your credibility and the value you offer.

- **Negotiation:** Exhibiting fairness and integrity during negotiations can fortify trust, encouraging prospects or clients to see long-term value in partnering with you beyond the immediate transaction.

- **Closing and follow-up:** Consistency in your follow-up and providing continued support reflect your dedication to client satisfaction and service excellence.

Your behavior is a cornerstone of your professional identity, influencing both your role within your organization and your effectiveness in client interactions. Align your actions with the core values you champion, and you'll not only enhance your credibility but also smooth the path for more successful outcomes. This direct alignment between your behavior and your professional ethos is what ultimately defines your impact as a leader.

COMMUNICATION: Effective communication in sales leadership is a nuanced art. It's not merely what you say, it's how you say it. Your tone, your choice of words, and the clarity with which you express complex ideas can alleviate stress or, if mishandled, exacerbate it.

Think of it this way: your visual appearance opens the door, but your communication invites others in, offering them a seat at the table in an otherwise challenging sales environment. Imagine you're presenting a strategic sales plan. Your crisp look of leadership sets a professional tone, but it's your persuasive communication that will be remembered. You choose words that inspire, not just inform. You explain; you don't just direct. You listen—truly listen—not only to respond but also to understand and to connect.

In these critical moments your ability to communicate with compassion and clarity can make all the difference in how your sales leadership is perceived. Your communication is the audible manifestation of your leadership. It's a vital component that, when in harmony with your appearance, establishes you as a leader who is not only seen but also heard and understood.

As a sales leader, the way you communicate defines not only the clarity of your message but also the depth of your relationships and the effectiveness of your influence. Effective communication in sales isn't just about what you say, it's deeply rooted in how you say it. Your tone, your choice of words, and your ability to convey complex ideas can dramatically impact your interactions and outcomes.

Your communication skills are the audible manifestation of your leadership that bridges the gap between challenges and solutions, making it a critical component in shaping how your leadership is perceived, both within your organization and in client interactions. Here are some examples:

- **Prospecting and initial contact:** At this initial stage, the professionalism and respect embedded in your communication set the foundational tone for the relationship. It's here that you begin to establish trust, a critical element that invites prospects or clients to further engage.

- **Needs assessment:** By focusing on understanding rather than responding, you demonstrate a commitment to the client's specific challenges and goals. This deep listening helps build a significant rapport, laying the groundwork for a strong, solution-oriented partnership.

- **Presentation and proposal:** How you communicate during your presentation or proposal can significantly impact your perceived credibility and the perceived value of your offerings. Confidence in your communication—not just in what you say but in the assured way you say it—reinforces your expertise and the benefits of your proposal.

- **Negotiation:** The communication style you adopt in negotiations can greatly influence the outcome. Fairness, integrity, and clarity in your discussions reinforce the client's perception of you as a trustworthy and ethical partner, encouraging them to consider the benefits of a relationship with you beyond the immediate transaction.

- **Closing and follow-up:** Consistency in communication during the closing and subsequent follow-up reflects your dedication to client satisfaction and service excellence. It's about reinforcing the relationship and ensuring that the client feels valued and supported, even after the deal is closed. This ongoing communication not only solidifies existing relationships but also opens doors to future opportunities.

In all these stages, your communication is more than just a transfer of information, it's an expression of your leadership and a reflection of your commitment to client success. By maintaining a high standard of communication throughout the sales cycle you not only enhance your interactions but also strengthen your reputation as a leader who is dedicated to positive and productive client relationships.

Remember: in the nuanced world of sales, your communication can open doors—or close them. Let your words, tone, and attentiveness to dialogue invite others in, offering them a seat at the table in the competitive, often challenging environment of sales.

DIGITAL PRESENCE: Your digital presence, as you know, also reflects your reputation, your expertise, and your judgment. This digital reflection of you can either strengthen trust in your professional capabilities or raise doubts about your fitness as a sales leader.

As you navigate the complexities of your digital presence, it's essential to consider the emotional contexts in which your digital presence might be scrutinized. Your digital footprint is not limited to traditional working hours. It's conceivable that, while you're leading a sales meeting, those you aim to influence are looking you up online, possibly right there in the boardroom or during a break. They might come across your digital interactions, and what they find could shape their emotional response before they ever engage with you. Furthermore, in an era when remote work and virtual collaborations are commonplace, the limitations of digital communication become more pronounced. The nuances of body language, the subtleties of facial expressions, and the inflections of your voice are often diminished or distorted through a screen.

Your digital professional identity should not merely be a shadow of your in-person identity, it should be its affirmation. You need to ensure consistency between your digital presence and your physical presence to fortify your sales leadership narrative. This congruence in identity is crucial; it reassures and confirms to others that the leader they encounter online is the same one leading the charge in the boardroom or the sales community.

Your digital footprint serves as a continuous and pervasive representation of your leadership. It's an integral part of how you are perceived by prospects, clients, and colleagues alike, influencing your reputation. Here are some examples:

- **Influence on perception:** At every stage of the sales cycle, your digital footprint precedes you. Potential prospects or clients and partners will often encounter your digital persona before they meet you in person. The quality and consistency of your online content and interactions set the groundwork for expectations and trust.

- **Amplification of leadership:** Your online activities can amplify your leadership qualities, allowing you to showcase thought leadership and industry expertise. This aspect of your digital presence is especially potent during the prospecting and needs assessment phases when first impressions are formed and opportunities for engagement are identified.

- **Continuity and consistency:** Throughout the sales cycle the congruence of your digital presence with your in-person interactions reassures prospects or clients of your authenticity. This consistency is crucial during negotiations and closing phases where trust is paramount.

- **Enhancing client relationships:** Your digital interactions can enhance relationships by providing additional touchpoints for engagement. Whether it's through timely responses on social media, insightful blog posts, or engaging online discussions, these interactions contribute to a deeper connection to and understanding of your prospects or clients.

- **Navigating the sales cycle remotely:** In scenarios where direct contact is limited—such as in virtual sales or remote client management—your digital presence becomes the primary avenue for interaction. It must effectively convey the nuances of your communication and behavior that would traditionally be communicated in person.

Thus, your digital footprint should be viewed as a component of your professional identity and as a strategic asset in your leadership tool kit. Your footprint enhances your visibility and influence across all stages of the sales cycle, reinforcing your role as a leader who not only adapts to modern challenges but also leverages digital platforms to forge stronger, more resilient client relationships. This holistic integration of your digital persona into your leadership approach is essential for maintaining efficacy and integrity in today's digitally driven marketplace.

ENVIRONMENT: Every choice you make, from the car you drive to the books on your office shelves, contributes to the tapestry of your professional identity. Each decision, even if seemingly unrelated to your professional responsibilities, can color the perception others have of you and that they may leverage, particularly in emotionally charged situations.

Consider, for instance, the vehicle you choose. It's not merely a means of transportation; it's a reflection of your values. An older, poorly maintained car might inadvertently convey to team members a disregard for modern efficiency, potentially fostering doubts about your organizational skills or resource management.

Conversely, a luxury sports car might lead to assumptions of extravagance, which could cause prospects, clients, or colleagues to question your financial judgment. It's those nuanced, emotional judgments that could reinforce preexisting notions, particularly in moments when trust and sales leadership are most crucial.

Think also of the individuals you associate with—friends, family, colleagues. They can reflect on you, positively or negatively. You may be judged by the company you keep, so it's prudent to surround yourself with people who amplify your professional identity.

As a sales leader, every element of your environment, from the physical space in which you work to the personal choices you make, contributes significantly to your professional identity and influences perceptions at every stage of the sales cycle. Here are some examples:

- **Physical environment and perception:** The layout and condition of your office project your values and operational style. An organized, aesthetically pleasing and functional workspace not only enhances your productivity but sends a clear message of professionalism and attention to detail, qualities revered in any leadership role. This perception is crucial during client visits and meetings when the environment directly influences client impressions.

- **Ambience and client experience:** The ambience of your office or meeting spaces plays a crucial role. Elements such as lighting, comfort, and accessibility contribute to the overall client experience. A well-thought-out ambience that caters to comfort and reflects your brand's ethos can help meetings be more engaging and productive. This is particularly influential when closing deals, as a comfortable and appealing environment can facilitate smoother interactions and more favorable outcomes.

- **Social environment and professional associations:** The professionals you associate with—colleagues, prospects, clients, and even friends—also reflect on you. The caliber of your associations can enhance or detract from your professional identity. In sales, where relationships and networks are crucial, the integrity of your colleagues can significantly bolster your own standing. This is especially important during collaborative efforts or when you are represented by your team in various settings.

- **Environmental consistency across touchpoints:** Ensuring consistency in your environment across all physical touchpoints reinforces your professional narrative. This consistency builds and maintains trust. It reassures prospects, clients, and colleagues of your authenticity and commitment to quality in every aspect of your professional life.

Every aspect of your life contributes to the overarching narrative of who you are as a sales leader and how the assumptions of others either support or challenge you in your leadership journey. The situations you navigate may differ, but the emotional undercurrents of judgment and perception are universal, influencing how you are seen and understood in your role.

Chapter 8
Leadership in a Digital Landscape

The More You Share, the More They Discover.
The Less You Share, the More Suspicion You Invite.

Chapter 8: Leadership in a Digital Landscape

In the vast expanse of the digital landscape, the rules of leadership presentation have undergone a seismic shift. The advent of the internet, followed by the ubiquity of social media and the increase of virtual encounters, has redefined the parameters. For sales leaders across all fields, the pivot from a primarily physical presence to a digital one is not just a transition, it's a transformation that requires a savvy understanding of how to navigate this new virtual territory.

Gone are the days when the measure of a sales leader was taken primarily by a sophisticated look, through a firm handshake, or direct eye contact. Today, it's the digital handshake, be it a LinkedIn profile, a professional bio on a company website, a glance through a webcam, or an introductory email. This digital first encounter can be influential enough to impact decisions and perceptions long before any face-to-face interaction occurs.

The digital portrait of today's sales leader must be as meticulously crafted as the physical presentation is. A hastily composed profile, a poorly chosen picture, or an unprofessional post can significantly impact your professional reputation. Search engines act as the new background check, and your online identity speaks volumes, setting the stage for all future interactions. In this age, it's the digital breadcrumb trail that leads others to your professional doorstep . . . or not. It forms the narrative of who you are, what you represent, and how you conduct your professional life.

A well-managed digital presence can open doors and establish a narrative of expertise and trustworthiness. Neglect it, and you may find that the narrative is written without your consent, shaped by others' interpretations and the whims of algorithms. The stakes are high. A sales leader's digital presence can be the deciding factor in a client's choice, the turning point in a potential team member's decision to join your ranks, or the catalyst for a partnership that propels your organization forward.

Your digital presence has the power to bolster or undermine the hard-earned emblems of your professional identity and standing. As such, it's imperative that you not only adapt to this digital evolution but embrace it with the same level of precision and dedication you would apply to any professional endeavor.

- **Internal impact:** Your digital footprint carries significant weight in shaping how you are perceived within the organization. A robust digital presence that showcases leadership, strategic thinking, and industry engagement can inspire confidence and respect among your team members. It can set a benchmark for professional standards within the team and foster a culture of continuous learning and digital engagement. Conversely, a neglected or inconsistent digital profile may lead to doubts about your leadership relevancy and adaptability in a tech-driven world. This aspect of your digital identity helps in molding the internal narrative about your leadership, influencing team morale and internal collaboration dynamics.

- **External impact:** Externally, your digital footprint serves as a critical touchpoint for prospects, clients, and industry colleagues assessing your credibility and expertise. A well-curated digital presence that aligns with your business values and professional acumen can significantly sway client decisions and enhance trust in your leadership. It shapes how potential partners and prospects or clients perceive the reliability and forward-thinking of your business practices. In the decision-making process prospects or clients often seek reassurance, not just through direct interactions but by examining the digital personas of the leaders they choose to engage with. Thus, your digital engagements and the narrative they build play a pivotal role in determining business opportunities and partnerships.

Your intentional footprint and deliberate digital narratives: Every click, post, and interaction within your digital landscape is a brushstroke in the portrait of your professional identity. This intentional footprint is about crafting a narrative that resonates with your leadership style and professional goals. It includes the content you create, the networks you engage with, and the professional conduct you maintain online. These deliberate actions are your direct voice in the digital world, offering a narrative that speaks of your expertise, your professional journey, and your thought leadership.

Pause and reflect on the intentional echoes your online actions create. In the digital world, every click, post, and email contributes to the intentional aspect of your digital footprint. This footprint is a carefully crafted mosaic, each piece a deliberate action adding up to the sum of your online presence. The photograph you choose for professional networking sites, the insightful articles you publish on industry trends, the supportive comments you leave on forums, these are the brushstrokes of your intentional digital presence.

Your unintentional footprint and the silent echoes of digital presence: Contrary to the controlled narrative of the intentional footprint, the unintentional footprint consists of the passive signals your digital presence emits. These might include how frequently you update your professional profiles, the timeliness of your responses, or even the modernity of your digital tools. This digital body language can subtly influence perceptions of your engagement and relevancy.

Just like body language in personal interactions, these digital cues provide a backdrop against which your explicit actions are measured. They whisper tales of your dedication to staying current and responsive in a swiftly evolving digital era.

Think about the subtle, unintentional ripples your digital presence may be sending, because there's a counterpart to this explicit storytelling—your unintentional digital footprint. It's the digital equivalent of body language, the subconscious cues that speak volumes without uttering a single word. This footprint includes how often you engage online. Are your contributions sporadic or consistent? Do you engage in real-time discourse, or does your digital silence linger long after the conversation has moved on?

The state of your professional profiles and website also whispers secrets about your attention to detail and relevance in a rapidly evolving professional landscape. A profile with outdated information or a professional website with broken links can inadvertently suggest a disconnection from current trends and technologies. Your tech-savviness—or lack thereof—is apparent in the way you navigate digital tools and platforms. Do you leverage the latest features to enhance your service offering, or do you falter with the basics of digital communication? And let's not forget the omnipotent algorithms of search engines. Your visibility or absence on the first page of Google search results can significantly affect your perceived credibility and authority, delineating a picture of prominence or obscurity.

In any profession where trust and expertise are the cornerstones of leadership, both the intentional and unintentional aspects of your digital footprint must be carefully curated. The silent symphony of actions and inactions forms the backdrop against which your explicit digital engagements are set. It's the combination of the overt and the subtle that collectively composes the full digital score of a sales leader's online presence.

KNOW: Assessing the Scope of Your e-Shadow

The first step in managing your digital footprint is simply to know and understand what's out there about you. This initial phase requires a comprehensive analysis of your digital presence and use of search engines and social media platforms to gather an unfiltered view of how you appear to the outside world.

Engage in a methodical search of your name, including the most common typos, and your titles, supplemented by your industry, the name of your organization, or the industries you're connected with across all major search engines, such as Google, Bing, and Yahoo, to ensure thoroughness.

This step exposes the full scope of your online presence, revealing everything from professional milestones to personal moments that have found their way onto the digital stage.

To gain an unfiltered perspective of how the digital world perceives you, use incognito or private browsing modes, features available in most web browsers. This approach removes the personalization of search results, offering a clear, unbiased view of your digital footprint as it would be seen by someone encountering you online for the first time.

This step ensures you're not merely seeing a reflection shaped by your own online behavior but the raw image that's presented to the wider world.

Then proceed with an audit of your social media platforms. Begin with a critical assessment of your profile, profile pictures, and header images across platforms. These visual elements serve as the digital representation of your persona. They often make the first impression online before a word about you is read.

Ensure the images are not only professionally appropriate but that they convey a sense of your commitment to your field, whether through imagery that resonates with your industry or a simple, dignified portrait that speaks of competence and trust.

Next, examine your handles and bio descriptions as well as the content you've shared.

This includes posts, articles, comments, and even likes. Each piece of content should align with your professional values, highlighting your knowledge, dedication to your work, and engagement with the broader community and your industry. It's about more than just steering clear of potential pitfalls such as controversial statements or unprofessional behavior. It's about actively contributing to discussions and sharing insights that affirm your position as a thought leader and a reliable professional.

Equally crucial is the scrutiny of your connections. Remember: the company you keep can impact perceptions of your professional judgment and affiliations. This is just as true online. Ensure your network includes only trusted friends and colleagues, industry leaders, and organizations that hold respect within your industry. Doing so not only bolsters your professional identity but cultivates your feed with pertinent, current information, keeping you informed and actively engaged with the latest developments in your field.

Continue with your virtual meetings setup. For sales professionals today, these digital gatherings are not just a matter of convenience but are a critical component of business operations and team coordination. As such, ensuring a professional appearance and environment during virtual meetings is just as crucial as during in-person interactions. Consider the visual backdrop of your virtual meetings. A cluttered or distracting background can detract from the meeting's focus and diminish your perceived professionalism. Poor lighting can make it difficult for others to see you clearly, making communication less effective and potentially impacting the connection you're trying to establish. Audio quality is another critical aspect. Background noise can disrupt the flow of conversation and hinder clear communication. Use a high-quality microphone and consider wearing headphones to minimize external noise.

In the digital era, written communication forms the backbone of daily interactions. Beyond emails and text messages, sales professionals engage in a myriad of digital correspondence, including project management tools, client portals, professional forums, and even comments on relevant online articles or blogs. Each platform and message carries the weight of your professional identity and requires careful consideration.

And always keep in mind that in the interconnected world of digital communication, the reach and permanence of your clicks and words extend far beyond the immediate recipient. Sales professionals, entrusted with confidential information or representing their brands, must be especially vigilant. The potential for communications to travel unexpectedly is ever-present.

Emails can easily be forwarded, and a message crafted for a specific individual or group can quickly find its way into unintended inboxes. Social media posts, despite the illusion of control through privacy settings or the ability to delete them, carry the risk of becoming screenshots that are shared. Once something is shared publicly, or even with a restricted audience, there's no guarantee against the content being captured and redistributed.

Even virtual meetings have the risk of being recorded without explicit consent. Third-party tools can capture audio and visual feeds, making any shared information, casual remarks, or discussions vulnerable to unauthorized distribution.

REPAIR: Correcting Your Cyber Image

This stage involves taking active steps to rectify or mitigate any negative aspects of your online presence, the obvious problems. Whether it's unflattering comments, outdated images, misleading information, or more serious issues like unfounded allegations or the unauthorized release of information, taking decisive action is essential for maintaining your professional integrity.

When negative content is within your control, such as on your personal or professional social media profiles, websites, or blogs, addressing these issues can be relatively straightforward. This could mean removing or editing the content in question or updating profile details to better reflect your professional standing.

The challenge becomes greater when the adverse content resides on platforms or websites outside of your direct control. In those instances, the initial step is to contact the administrators or content creators, politely requesting the removal or correction of the content. Be clear about the content's negative impact on your professional identity.

If direct requests are unsuccessful, or if the content's removal is complex, it might be wise to engage reputation management professionals. These experts are skilled in strategies to de-emphasize negative content in search engine results, making it less visible or discoverable by those searching for you online.

During this phase you also should confront the not-so-obvious problems. These are instances when the search results about you are not outright negative but don't adequately showcase your achievements, expertise, or characteristics you wish to project. A search result that isn't damaging but fails to showcase your qualifications or contributions to your field can be equally limiting.

The strategy is twofold: enhancement and creation. Start by enhancing existing content. At the same time, focus on creating new content that reflects your professional identity. This can include publishing articles on reputable industry blogs, participating in interviews or podcasts pertinent to your area of expertise, or engaging in community initiatives that garner positive attention. Using social media platforms to share insights, joining professional discussions, and highlighting your contributions also can enrich the quality of your digital footprint.

Shaping the narrative around your digital presence is essential. Not only does it ensure your digital presence accurately reflects your real-world skills and values, it establishes you as a thought leader in your field. This proactive stance ensures that when prospects, clients, colleagues, or potential partners search for you online, they will encounter a comprehensive and affirmative portrayal of your professional identity.

OWN: Claiming Your Virtual Real Estate

To address a potential problem, owning your name online is not just a matter of professional branding, it's a strategic necessity. A potential challenge arises when individuals share your name, a not uncommon scenario. From celebrities dominating search engine results to name twins with a more active online presence, these situations can dilute your digital identity, making it harder for prospects, clients, business partners, or industry colleagues to find the real you.

To tackle this issue it's crucial to establish a distinctive digital presence that clearly identifies you. This could involve using your middle name or initials in your professional profiles, incorporating professional titles or credentials, or choosing a unique version of your name that's linked to your area of expertise.

These tweaks help ensure that searches for your name lead to you, not someone else. Additionally, these tweaks act as a safeguard against future issues. The ever-changing nature of the internet means new figures can suddenly become prominent, potentially eclipsing your online presence.

For example, if a new celebrity with your name emerges, they could take over search results. Or worse, someone with a negative reputation could impact the perception of your shared name. Establishing a unique online identity reduces those risks, keeping your professional achievements and reputation front and center.

This effort means going beyond merely setting up profiles on popular platforms such as LinkedIn or Instagram. It involves a comprehensive approach to claiming your name across all digital channels, ensuring that you, and only you, control how your name is represented online.

The process begins with registering your name on as many platforms, directories, and online forums as possible. Although it might seem daunting to maintain active profiles on each, the goal isn't necessarily to be active everywhere but to prevent others from assuming your identity or diluting your online presence.

By owning your name on these platforms, you create a protective barrier around your digital identity, making it harder for others to impersonate you or misrepresent your professional brand.

Furthermore, secure your domain name (e.g., YourName.com). Even if a personal website is not in your immediate plans, controlling your domain is a crucial part of digital ownership. It blocks others from capitalizing on your name and sets the stage for a centralized space for your professional portfolio.

Also, delve into niche platforms and professional directories. These channels enable you to claim your name in more specialized areas and improve your visibility among colleagues, acting as further validation of your professional identity and solidifying your standing within your professional community.

By taking these steps you help ensure that when you are searched for online, you will present a consistent narrative, showcasing the breadth of your professional life, visible not only to clients or team members but also the wider industry network.

CONTROL: Commanding Your Digital Boundaries

Taking control of your digital presence extends beyond just owning your name across various platforms. It includes meticulously managing the nuances of your online presence.

First, examine the privacy settings on all your social media profiles. Each platform offers a range of options that control who can see your posts, who can tag you, who can comment on or share your content, and even who can send you friend requests or follow you. It's essential to tailor those settings to suit your personal preferences and professional needs, ensuring your content is visible to the right audience while protecting your privacy.

Also consider the implications of your current connections, because they can reflect on your professional persona. Be mindful of the people you accept or seek out, because those connections can be viewed as an endorsement of your professional standards and network.

Moreover, be proactive in managing the content associated with your profile. Regularly review tags and mentions, removing or disassociating yourself from any content that doesn't align with your professional identity or privacy preferences. This might include untagging yourself from photos or asking colleagues to refrain from mentioning you in certain posts.

Additionally, think about the visibility of your likes, comments, and shares. These actions can be as telling as the content you post directly. They contribute to the overall narrative of your identity online, so it's wise to conduct these interactions with the same care and consideration you'd give to your own posts.

Finally, keep abreast of updates to privacy policies and settings on each platform. Social media sites frequently update their privacy features, and staying informed allows you to adjust your settings proactively, ensuring continuous control over your digital presence.

By taking these steps you not only protect your professional reputation but establish boundaries that respect your privacy and the privacy of those you interact with online. In an era when digital interactions can have real-world implications, such control is not just advisable, it's indispensable.

MONITOR: Persistent Surveillance of Your Online Self

The final step in managing your digital footprint is to vigilantly monitor your online presence. Regularly checking how you appear on the internet isn't an act of vanity but a critical component of professional reputation management. There's no harm and no shame in frequently searching for your name in search engines.

One effective strategy is to set up automated alerts. Most search engines offer this feature for free, sending you notifications whenever your name appears online. This proactive approach ensures you're always informed about your digital mentions, allowing you to address any new content quickly.

If you work in an industry where client reviews and testimonials are common across search engines, social media platforms, general review sites, or industry-specific platforms, make sure to consistently review those too. Publicly expressing gratitude for positive feedback not only reinforces the favorable aspects of your services but also motivates others to share their experiences.

Addressing negative comments is equally critical. Prompt and constructive responses to less favorable reviews demonstrate your commitment to valuing client input and to service improvement.

This approach is a chance to transform a challenging situation into a testament to your dedication to client satisfaction and service excellence.

In the fast-paced digital world, narratives can quickly spiral out of control if not addressed promptly. Being aware of what's being said about you online allows you to take timely action, whether it's correcting inaccuracies, responding to feedback, or updating your digital content to better reflect your professional identity.

And while it straddles a fine line in terms of privacy, keeping an eye on the digital activities of your team members also can be prudent.

Whether it's through email communication, virtual meetings, or interactions on various digital platforms, each digital touchpoint offers an opportunity for you to reinforce your professional identity. It's not enough to curate a strong social media presence or a professional website, every digital interaction must be approached with the same level of care and strategic thinking. This holistic approach to managing your digital identity not only safeguards your professional reputation but amplifies the positive impact you can have within your field.

Your look of leadership knows no bounds. It resonates through every pixel and screen and extends beyond the confines of your office walls, casting a digital silhouette as vast as your ambition.

Chapter 9
Leaders Lead by Example

By Changing Nothing,
Nothing Changes.

Chapter 9:
Leaders Lead by Example

Your paramount duty as a leader is not just to lead but to cultivate more leaders by demonstrating that exceptional leadership is less about dictating actions and more about setting a compelling example. By embodying the values and standards you wish to see, you become a leader others are inspired to follow. This approach is what distinguishes a leader from a manager. Whereas managers focus on ensuring tasks are completed by issuing directives and adhering to the letter of the law, leaders inspire action through their own choices. Leaders don't just tell their team what to do, they show them how it's done. Your actions send a powerful message of "Do as I do," fostering an environment of mutual respect and emulation.

Great sales leaders intuitively understand that leading by example is the most potent form of guidance, one that creates an unspoken standard that features an organic dress code, a blueprint for behavior, a benchmark for communication, a template for digital engagement, and a standard for the living and nonliving elements that you surround yourself with, all of which are far more influential than any written policy.

Your team members and colleagues are always observing, learning and, in many cases, emulating your actions. Being a sales leader means accepting that you're always on stage, setting an example for every person you interact with. And although it might sound obvious, it's crucial to ensure the example you're setting is a positive one every moment of every day.

By practicing what you preach and paying attention to the minutiae of your professional identity, you not only enhance your leadership but inspire your team to strive for the same excellence.

The flip side, being a poor role model, is the easiest way to undermine your own authority as a sales leader. Does that mean you have to follow all the rules (and burdens) your organization puts on you? Maybe. Does that mean you can't have your own style and can't stand out and show your personality? Absolutely not.

Influential sales leaders are confident, and they trust themselves enough to live their own interpretation of a professional identity. They've put so much thought into it and created such a defined professional identity that their presence is instantly felt when they enter the room. They're mindful of how others could perceive them and of how they want to be perceived.

If part of this professional identity-building requires sales leaders to wear denims, they wear denims. If wearing sneakers with their suit adds something unique to their defined professional identity, they wear sneakers. Influential sales leaders exude confidence and trust in their ability to craft a distinct professional identity that resonates with who they are.

Courageous sales leaders don't make excuses. Instead, they apologize when they've made a mistake. And, usually, people have the most respect for those who don't hesitate to say, "I'm sorry" or "I was wrong."

But people have a hard time respecting those who look for excuses in advance. An effective sales leader makes commitments, not excuses. If team members see a sales leader who embodies commitment and courage, one who takes responsibility for their actions and choices, those team members feel safe to follow that leader.

And the same is true for your team members. When it comes to their visual appearance, you might be faced with a variety of excuses. Sometimes they might claim it's too hot or too cold to dress appropriately, letting the climate dictate their professional standards.

Financial concerns also may play a role with some feeling the pinch of investing in a high-quality wardrobe or grappling with guilt over such spending.

Time, that ever-elusive commodity, is another barrier with the hustle of daily life seeming to leave little room for meticulous planning. Amid those justifications, a deeper thread of resistance emerges. A claimed lack of style sense becomes a shield against change, and the actions of other team members—"They do it too"—serve as misguided validation.

Geographic excuses, such as "We're in the suburbs, not Manhattan," highlight a misunderstanding that professionalism has a zip code. Venturing into the digital world, some diminish the importance of a professional digital presence with a wave of the hand, dismissing it as "just the internet." This miscalculation overlooks the profound impact of digital impressions in today's interconnected world.

These excuses, although varied, share a common theme: they suggest that professionalism is confined to a specific weather forecast, price tag, or locale. As a leader you might find yourself entangled in a web of excuses dangling through the corridors as team members at all levels seek loopholes in the standards that might justify their choices. In this landscape of justifications, your role as a sales leader is crucial. Successful leaders sidestep these excuses to send a clear message—professionalism is nonnegotiable because it is integral to the fabric of the organization and essential for individual and collective success.

The Leader's Challenge: It's Not You, It's Someone Else

Sending a clear message to team members sometimes means having honest conversations with your team about sensitive topics that can range from inappropriate clothing to personal hygiene issues, from mismanagement of emotions to unfortunate social media posts, from neglecting workspaces to disrespecting stakeholders.

Although such discussions may feel uncomfortable, they're integral to maintaining the professional integrity your role demands. And it's not uncommon for sales leaders to feel apprehensive about raising such subjects. Do you feel like that? Maybe it's because of . . .

- Your commitment to fostering a positive team environment, knowing harmony is pivotal to operational success.

- An inclination to avoid causing emotional distress, given your role, which may be centered on support and development.

- Concern over adverse reactions that could disrupt team cohesion.

- The need to exercise authority while maintaining a non-confrontational stance to preserve a cooperative team spirit.

- A tendency to avoid uncomfortable situations, particularly in a setting where team members work closely and collaboratively.

- The difficulty in finding the right words to express your concerns.

- Thinking you are entering a personal space by addressing these issues.

But please remember that your primary goal is to support your team members' professional development, not to criticize them personally. Here's how you can approach these delicate conversations with confidence and clarity.

Begin by thoroughly preparing for the discussion. It's crucial to enter these conversations with a clear understanding of the issue. Start by identifying the problem with precision. Reflect on the consequences this problem creates, not just for the individual involved but for the entire team, prospects, clients, and the organization as a whole. If it doesn't affect anyone, there's no need for a conversation at all. Determine who is directly responsible for the issue. It's essential to pinpoint when the issue first arose and assess its frequency. Reflect on previous attempts to address the problem and their outcomes. This preparation helps you approach the conversation with a solid foundation, making it easier to discuss potential solutions effectively. Finally, assess whether this is a conversation you should have independently or if it would benefit from the presence of another party, such as a human resources representative or a senior colleague. This decision should be based on the nature of the issue, its sensitivity, and the potential impact on the individual or team.

Seek guidance before you approach. In any case it's recommended you consult with human resources or a legal advisor, if you have access to such a resource, because some issues carry legal implications and require a delicate approach. Before diving into conversations about sensitive topics such as alcohol, drugs, religion, sex, violence, theft, fraud, harassment, or bullying, it's wise to consult an expert who can provide essential guidance on handling the situation correctly, inform you about any disciplinary actions that may be appropriate, and ensure that you adhere to laws and policies. Seeking such advice serves as a protective measure for both you and your organization and helps prevent potential missteps that could lead to false accusations or lawsuits. Addressing such matters without proper preparation and understanding of the legal context could, inadvertently, cause significant harm.

Choose the best time and space. Selecting the appropriate setting for such a delicate conversation is critical, especially within the bustling environment of corporate offices or similar settings. These kinds of conversations should never occur in public spaces, like hallways, where there's a risk of being overheard or observed, compromising the privacy and dignity of the team member involved. Instead, opt for a quiet, private space where confidentiality can be maintained—perhaps your office or a secluded meeting room. This environment ensures both you and the team member feel secure, won't be distracted, and can speak openly.

Additionally, choosing the right moment can significantly impact the receptiveness and outcome of the discussion. Avoid scheduling such talks during peak operational hours or just before or after stressful meetings, because stress levels and distractions can hinder the effectiveness of your message. Instead, find a time when both you and the team member are least likely to be under immediate pressure, allowing for a more focused, calm, and constructive exchange. Also, you don't want to have to rush through this conversation, because doing so could lead to misunderstandings or the feeling that the issue isn't being taken seriously.

Bring yourself into the right mindset. Remember that these conversations are not personal attacks against your team member. Instead, they're meant to be constructive and help your team member, your team, and the whole organization improve. In addition, please remember that neither of you is probably looking forward to this conversation. It's likely your team member is just as anxious as you are. So take a few minutes to clear your head and remind yourself of the objective.

Start the conversation with positive reinforcement. Doing so instantly reaffirms your team member's value, especially if you share praise about measurable achievements. This praise could include citing specific instances in which their attention to detail improved project outcomes, their quick thinking averted a potential crisis, or their insights led to a significant reduction of costs.

Conversely, vague compliments like "You're doing great" or "We appreciate your hard work" lack the specificity to make the individual feel genuinely recognized. Such statements, although well-intentioned, fail to highlight the unique contributions of the team member and can be used against you: "Well, you said I'm doing great, so what's your point?" Focusing on concrete achievements sets a constructive tone and demonstrates that you value their contributions in a specific area while allowing that there may be room for improvement in another area.

Use neutral and straightforward language. When addressing concerns it's crucial to be clear and precise to ensure there's no room for misunderstanding. For instance, instead of saying, "Your outfits are inappropriate," you need to specify, "I've noticed that your wardrobe choices, particularly in terms of interaction with prospects or clients, may not align with our company's expectations. This is especially true when you wear xyz." This approach makes your feedback not only more actionable but also less personal. In addition, aim for a delivery that is straightforward and unembellished yet sensitive. Let the facts speak for themselves, and calmly present them without the distortion of emotional undercurrents. Doing so helps ensure your input is received as intended, as a means to maintain professional standards and uphold the organization's reputation rather than as a personal attack.

Don't refer to others. When you need to address a concern with a team member, center the conversation on your own observations and experiences rather than on third-party comments or hearsay. It's crucial to base your conversation on incidents you've witnessed personally, not on anecdotes or grievances passed on by others. If the situation occurred in your absence or cannot be personally verified, it's vital to have written, verifiable evidence to substantiate your points. This approach not only preserves your team member's dignity but also strengthens the trust between you, the team member, and your team.

Describe the consequences for the team member and your organization. Articulate the impact on the team member's own reputation and the broader impact of their actions. For instance, explain how their choices not only hamper their own professional growth but also tarnish the collective reputation of the team, department, and organization. This perspective shift helps the team member understand the gravity of the situation beyond their individual sphere. For example, constant tardiness might not only affect their workload but also strain team dynamics and departmental efficiency. But be sure to address your concerns without making it about your personal grievances (i.e., "I" statements). The focus should remain on the consequences of their actions on themselves and the organization, not on you as an individual leader. This ensures the feedback is purposeful and targeted toward fostering an environment in which their own well-being and the highest levels of organizational excellence are maintained.

Be clear about how you would like them to change. Rather than dwell on the past, move quickly to the future. But don't expect your team member to know exactly what you expect them to change. For instance, if a team member has been inconsistent in meeting project deadlines, don't just highlight those delays. Instead, clearly outline the steps for improvement, such as adhering to a timeline for task completion, providing exact dates, and announcing regular progress updates. Specify that these measures are nonnegotiable for maintaining the high standards of productivity and professionalism your team is committed to. Unless you're specific in your request, there will be confusion about what needs to be done (or not) moving forward.

Be careful when offering support. Although it's essential to be supportive, emphasize that the responsibility for improvement rests with the team member. You should be there to assist, but the obligation is on them. This stance prevents dependency and promotes accountability.

Be prepared for pushback. In fact, anticipate it. It's a natural response. But it's crucial to maintain your composure and keep the dialogue centered on the issue. Instead of allowing their response to sidetrack the conversation, seize it as a chance to emphasize your expectations and the importance of meeting them. Instead of leaping to rigidly defend your stance, pause and hear what your team member articulates. Misunderstandings, fear, or frustration often underpin the team member's responses. Your attentiveness not only demonstrates respect for their viewpoint, it also can diffuse tensions, paving the way for a dialogue that's both more constructive and collaborative. Although you can acknowledge their emotions as a way to navigate their initial reactions, seize the moment to again clarify the issue, the solution you discussed, and the impact it has. By reiterating the conversation's objective—to foster their development and enhance overall outcomes—you underscore the collective aim of this exchange. Finally, remember that your conversation is not a personal critique, and their reaction is not an attack on you.

Summarize what was discussed and announce a follow-up. As you draw the conversation to a close, it's essential to encapsulate the key points discussed. This summarization isn't just about reiterating the issues but about confirming the mutual understanding and commitment to the agreed-upon actions. It's a moment to ensure no detail is lost and that both parties are aligned in their expectations and responsibilities. Announcing a follow-up or a check-in at a specific date is the next critical step, one that underscores your dedication to the process, the individual's progress, and the overall success of your organization. But this intent carries weight only if it's fulfilled. Failing to follow through not only diminishes the effectiveness of the initial conversation but erodes your authority and credibility.

End the conversation on a neutral note. The way in which such a conversation concludes can significantly influence the subsequent actions and attitudes of your team member. It's essential to strike the right balance in the closing moments, ensuring the team member doesn't leave feeling overly discouraged or burdened by the discussion. Conversely, ending on an excessively optimistic note might dilute the importance of the feedback you have given, a phenomenon I refer to as "sandwich" feedback. When the critical message is sandwiched between two positives, it may lessen the negative impact. Aim for a neutral closure such as "Let's go back to work," which signals the specific discussion is complete and is just one of many you experience as a leader.

Document the exchange. This ensures there is a clear record, safeguarding both you and your organization against future disputes regarding performance or conduct. Start by documenting who was present at the meeting, then capture the full context of the discussion. It's vital to include the date, time, and location to anchor the conversation in a specific moment and place. Next, meticulously record the substance of the meeting. What issues were discussed? This includes the initial observations that prompted the conversation, the feedback you provided, and the team member's response. Crucially, detail the agreed-upon actions, including who is responsible for what and the timelines for those actions. This clarity prevents any ambiguity about expectations and responsibilities, ensuring everyone is aligned on the path forward. Also, outline the expected outcomes of those actions. What changes or improvements should result from this intervention? This sets a clear benchmark for assessing progress and effectiveness. Finally, specify the follow-up steps, including who will carry them out and when. Documenting these aspects creates a comprehensive and indisputable record of the conversation. And this thoroughness underscores the gravity with which you, as a sales leader, approach your role, demonstrating a commitment to fairness, transparency, and the growth of your team.

There also may be instances when you encounter a situation that falls outside your direct span of authority. Perhaps you're leading a project with team members who don't directly report to you, or you're in a matrix organization in which your influence is more lateral than vertical.

In such cases it's not recommended that you have this kind of conversation. Instead, engage with the individual's direct leaders or with those who have direct authority and share your observations and concerns, preferably with documentation that underscores your concern. Present the issue not as criticism but as an opportunity for collective improvement, emphasizing the shared mission of providing exceptional service. In these delicate scenarios your role as a sales leader is to facilitate positive change indirectly, using your influence to advocate for standards that align with the organization's values and objectives. It's a dance of diplomacy that requires patience, empathy, and a strategic understanding of organizational dynamics.

As you can see, sales leadership is a journey filled with a variety of challenges and responsibilities. It demands courage to engage in difficult conversations, wisdom to navigate the limitations of your authority, and the vision to see beyond immediate issues toward the greater goal of positive change. Always remember that the true mark of leadership is not just in wielding authority but in inspiring growth, fostering resilience, and leading by example, especially when the path is complex.

Chapter 10
Moving Forward

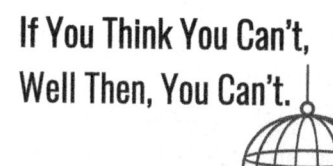

If You Think You Can't,
Well Then, You Can't.

Chapter 10: Moving Forward

In concluding our journey through leadership and the crafting of your professional identity, it's essential to recognize that enhancing your professional identity is not merely for personal gratification, it's a fundamental aspect of your professional development. This endeavor brings rewards that extend well beyond the surface. It inspires trust within your network, cohesion within your team, and opportunities for career progression. The critical question then shifts from whether you should refine your professional identity to the depth of your commitment to ongoing improvement and the pursuit of excellence. In the dynamic landscape of any sales industry where challenges and prospects exist side by side, the need to distinguish yourself for the right reasons is paramount. The capacity to set yourself apart through an outstanding professional identity is what differentiates true sales leaders. These leaders establish an identity that aligns with the values and goals of their organizations, meet the expectations of their stakeholders, support the ambitions of their teams and, of course, value themselves as the great leaders they are.

This book has aimed to guide you through the nuanced dance of this professional identity, blending the science of first impressions with the art of a sustained imprint. From the subtle cues conveyed by your look of leadership to the profound influence of digital footprints, many aspects of your professional identity have been dissected, offering you a blueprint for intentional self-presentation.

Now, about that potato chip on the cover. Did you notice?

At first glance it may seem like a whimsical choice for a book dedicated to such a serious topic. Yet it serves as a powerful metaphor for the concept of identity, personal and professional alike.

Imagine we're embarking on a journey together through a bustling supermarket. As we navigate the aisles, our attention is drawn to the myriad of products vying for our attention. The significance of packaging design becomes strikingly apparent—the strategic placement of brands and the few critical seconds that influence our decision to add an item to our shopping cart or pass it by. It's in those moments that the familiarity of a trusted brand effortlessly convinces us to make a purchase whereas the allure of a new product demands our notice through meticulously crafted packaging designed to leave a lasting first impression.

Consider the relationship between a product and its packaging. Although they are often perceived as separate entities, the most impactful packaging designs demonstrate that thoughtful packaging can not only complement but enhance the product within. The packaging's shape, size, colors, and imagery are meticulously chosen to influence you to buy the product inside.

Now, let's pause in front of the snack aisle and stare at the hundreds of potato chip packages. Chip packaging offers fascinating insights into successful branding. Do you realize that every potato chip packaging has an image of a chip on the front? Perhaps you've noticed the most successful chip brands communicate this clear promise: "What you see is what you get." The imagery shows perfectly shaped potato chips, an image that conveys the product's appeal more than any verbal description could. It's straightforward. It shows the product in its most enticing form.

Yet, as you know, there's a twist. The crumbled reality inside the bag doesn't match the perfection depicted on the outside. Despite not having a transparent section to preview the contents, we're drawn in by the promise of ideal, unbroken chips. Again and again we continue to buy them, even though we're aware of the illusion.

The Image of Leadership in Sales

The lesson is profound: a compelling external presentation can lead people to embrace you, even if the internal reality doesn't quite match. Achieving the opposite effect is significantly more challenging.

For sales leaders, the metaphor of potato chip packaging is a poignant one for the importance of a consistent professional identity. You must ensure that your external presentation—your appearance, behavior, communication, digital presence, and work environment—reflects you in the best light.

Just as the chip bag's imagery promises a certain experience, sales leaders must convey an identity that their teams and stakeholders can instantly respect and trust. Although no leader is without flaws—comparable to the mix of whole and broken chips within a bag—it's the strategic depiction of your competencies and commitment that should be emphasized. Over time, just as consumers come to accept the imperfect contents of a chip bag due to their trust in the brand, so too will others accept a leader's human flaws if they are convinced of the leader's dedication to their role and the success of the team.

Now let's take another look at the aisle of potato chips and contemplate expectations. If I were to ask you to pick a spicy flavor of chips, most people would subconsciously look for a red bag. Want an organic variant? Then you'd probably look for a green or brown bag.

Our brains are wired to associate specific colors and designs with certain product attributes. This principle of expectation extends beyond the supermarket aisle to the realm of sales leadership. Just as we have predefined notions about product packaging, we harbor expectations about a sales leader's professional identity.

Despite the diversity in sales leadership styles and personalities, certain universal expectations remain consistent. Just as the bold red packaging of spicy chips stands out to a shopper looking for flavor, sales leaders who align their presentation with professional norms are easily recognized and trusted.

There's certainly space for individuality and a break from convention, like a neon-pink chip bag among the typical reds and greens. A sales leader might also choose to deviate from traditional visual cues through distinctive clothing or an unconventional approach. This differentiation can attract attention, drawing those intrigued by novelty and innovation. But it may also miss the mark of subconscious expectations, posing a challenge to immediate recognition as a leader in their professional field. Much like a shopper instinctively reaching for the familiar red bag, oblivious to a pink option, people often gravitate toward the comfort of what they know, traditional emblems of authority and expertise.

Finally, like well-established potato chip brands that are strategically positioned at eye level on shelves to be easily seen and chosen, influential sales leaders naturally command a presence and often enjoy higher recognition. Conversely, less prominent brands—or sales leaders—might need to exert more effort to be noticed.

In a competitive sales environment, being at eye level signifies remaining at the forefront of your managers' and all stakeholders' minds, always ready to be selected for your visible dedication to excellence, professionalism, and service. This prominence isn't merely physical but extends to the entire professional identity you construct as a sales leader.

As this chapter closes, let the lasting lesson be the craft of your professional identity, the external manifestation of your inner capabilities. Let the professional identity you create stand as your unwavering representative by conveying expertise, fostering trust, and managing the intricacies of sales leadership with poise.

Your "packaging" is not merely an aesthetic choice, it's a strategic tool that, when aligned with your skills and vision, can weather the storms of challenge and change, so let it amplify your strengths, not overshadow them.

As you move forward, may your professional identity resonate with intention, your sales leadership echo with impact, and your presence be felt, even in silence.

Stand out not just to be seen but to make a difference, to inspire trust, and to drive progress.

Here's to the sales leader in you, packaged to perfection, poised for greatness, and perpetually ready to turn challenges into opportunities.

Go forth and lead, not just with authority but with the magnetism of a well-crafted identity, one that's as compelling and multifaceted as the leader within you.

Acknowledgments

To you, the reader:

This book is a testament to your journey, your challenges, and your triumphs. You might have reached for this book seeking guidance, inspiration, or affirmation in your role within the dynamic world of sales. Whatever your reason, I want to acknowledge you.

Thank you for choosing a path that demands a unique blend of resilience, adaptability, and empathy. For every client you have guided, for every relationship you have nurtured, for every moment you chose perseverance over resignation, thank you. Your drive and dedication have not gone unnoticed. You carry with you not just the responsibility of meeting targets but the privilege of shaping client experiences and driving business growth.

I'm grateful for your unwavering integrity and your ethical compass that navigates you through the complexities of the sales landscape. I'm inspired by your determination to push the boundaries of what's possible and to innovate for the sake of your prospects, clients, and organization.

Thank you for being the bridge between products and people, for being the voice that articulates value and the ears that listen to client needs. Your ability to navigate challenging conversations, to find common ground, and to build trust is remarkable. And for your constant striving to elevate the sales profession, to challenge stereotypes, and to redefine what it means to be a sales leader, my gratitude knows no bounds.

To the sales leaders who mentor and guide aspiring professionals, who share their wisdom and experience generously, thank you. Your investment in the next generation of sales leaders is shaping the future of the profession.

To the sales professionals who balance the demands of their role with their commitments to family, friends, and personal and professional development, I see you. Your ability to juggle multiple priorities and still bring your best self to your work is admirable.

As you close this book, remember that the recognition of your work, your commitment, and your leadership extends far beyond these pages. It's reflected in the prospects or clients you serve, the teams you lead, the organizations you elevate, and the industries you influence.

With respect and admiration,
Sylvie di Giusto

About the Author

International keynote speaker Sylvie di Giusto brings her expertise from a successful corporate career in Europe to every presentation. Formerly the head of a management academy and innovation hub, she developed innovative leadership programs for high-end education with unprecedented training methods. As the chief of staff for the chief human resources officer of Europe's largest tourism and retail group, Sylvie coordinated all group-wide human resources teams and activities. Prior to that, at a consultancy firm she implemented online and in-person training and development initiatives for Fortune 100 companies.

Extraordinary professionals at respected organizations around the world including American Express, American Airlines, Hilton, Nespresso, Microsoft, Prudential, and even the US Air Force trust Sylvie to help them make the right decisions to grow their brands and bottom lines. Building on her five cornerstones of modern emotional intelligence—visual, behavioral, verbal, digital, and social—Sylvie gives her audiences Power of Choice, a conscious decision-making framework that allows us to understand our perceptions, choose our behaviors, and determine our best outcomes.

Sylvie is the author of *The Image of Leadership, Discover Your Fair Advantage,* and the upcoming *Make Me Feel Important.* Sylvie takes audiences on an entertaining, spectacular, and thought-provoking journey through the brain and mind, from the unconscious to the conscious and, ultimately, to the heights of personal, professional, and organizational success.

For speaking engagements, please contact Sylvie's wonderful team at sylviebookings@cmispeakers.com or call +1-403-398-8488.

Perception Audit

Take the free Perception Audit and unveil the image you project to the world in just fifteen minutes. Receive a personalized report that illuminates how others perceive your professional identity and learn to align your self-view with the impression you intend to make.

Are you ready to meet the YOU that everyone else sees?

Or visit sylviedigiusto.com/audit.

After you've gained the clarity you need to polish your professional identity and project the best version of you in the workplace and beyond, let's stay connected. Follow me on social media to join the conversation about *The Image of Leadership for Sales.*

- instagram.com/sylviedigiusto
- linkedin.com/in/sylviedigiusto
- facebook.com/sylviedigiusto
- youtube.com/c/sylviedigiusto
- tiktok.com/@sylviedigiusto

Your Voice and Our Collective Reach

Books—just like you—face perception challenges.

In a world where perception is reality, the value and impact of books are often judged by the quantity and quality of their Amazon reviews. So if this book has offered new perspectives or valuable insights, please consider sharing your experience online. Your review not only helps shape the book's impact but also guides others to find the same resource you did.

Your role in this narrative could just be the beginning.

For those who have found resonance within these pages and wish to spread the wisdom within their team or organization, I offer preferred customer pricing for bulk orders. Please reach out to my wonderful team at sylviebookings@cmispeakers.com or call +1-403-398-8488. Let's empower more leaders together.

Made in the USA
Middletown, DE
27 July 2024